Healthcare, Frugal Innovation,
and Professional Voluntarism

Helen Louise Ackers • James Ackers-Johnson • John Chatwin • Natasha Tyler

# Healthcare, Frugal Innovation, and Professional Voluntarism

## A Cost-Benefit Analysis

Helen Louise Ackers
Social Sciences
University of Salford
Salford, Lancashire, United Kingdom

James Ackers-Johnson
Directorate of Social Sciences
University of Salford
Salford, Lancashire, United Kingdom

John Chatwin
School of Nursing, Midwifery, Social
   Work & Social Sciences
University of Salford
Salford, Lancashire, United Kingdom

Natasha Tyler
School of Nursing, Midwifery, Social
   Work & Social Sciences
University of Salford
Salford, Lancashire, United Kingdom

ISBN 978-3-319-48365-8          ISBN 978-3-319-48366-5 (eBook)
DOI 10.1007/978-3-319-48366-5

Library of Congress Control Number: 2017933688

This Palgrave Macmillan imprint is published by Springer Nature
The registered company is Springer International Publishing AG
The registered company address is: Gewerbestrasse 11, 6330 Cham, Switzerland

# ACKNOWLEDGEMENTS

We would like to acknowledge the support, both financial and personal, that we have received from the Tropical Health and Education Trust which made the Sustainable Volunteering Project (SVP) possible. We would also like to thank Health Education England (HEE) for supporting the MOVE project, which provided the resource to broaden the research and further explore the returns to professional volunteers from placements in low resource settings.[1]

Our gratitude extends to all of the professional volunteers who have so generously engaged with the SVP evaluation and MOVE study and played such an active role as co-researchers in project development and evaluation.

## NOTE

1. The Sustainable Volunteering Project (SVP) is funded by the Tropical Health and Education Trust (THET) as part of the Health Partnership Scheme, which is itself supported by the UK Department for International Development (DFID). The views expressed are those of the authors and do not necessarily reflect the views of THET or HEE.

# CONTENTS

# LIST OF FIGURES

# LIST OF TABLES

# CHAPTER 1

# International Mobility and Learning in the UK National Health Service

**Abstract** This chapter sets the study of international placements for healthcare professionals in the wider context of knowledge mobilisation characterising mobile health workers as knowledge brokers. It then discusses the concept of 'volunteer' and how appropriate this term is to the study of placement learning. The term 'professional volunteer' is proposed as a compromise. Two key contextual dimensions are then outlined: first, global health and the needs of low-resource settings. Secondly, the challenges facing a resource constrained UK National Health Service.

**Keywords** International mobility · Training · UK National Health Service

Internationalisation has become a feature of many, if not most, careers. It can be achieved through a variety of mechanisms, including, perhaps most obviously, the recruitment of staff from other countries. Certainly, international mobility has come to play an important role both in terms of attracting the 'brightest and best' across global labour markets (Iredale 2001; Mahroum 2000; Smetherham et al. 2010) and in terms of fostering mechanisms to provide international exposure to locally recruited staff. Mobilities of various forms involving shorter or longer stays at different stages in careers and to diverse locations are widely acknowledged to play an important role in the generation and exploitation of knowledge and

H.L. Ackers et al., *Healthcare, Frugal Innovation, and Professional Voluntarism*, DOI 10.1007/978-3-319-48366-5_1

innovation. Whilst the 'mobility imperative' (Ackers 2010; Cox 2008) has received greatest attention in those careers specifically associated with knowledge generation (such as research), there is increasing recognition that all professionals are inherently engaged in knowledge creation and mobilisation (Baruch and Hall 2004; Baruch and Reis 2015; DeFillippi and Arthur 1994).

Healthcare professionals are not simply the consumers or users of knowledge but through their daily lives actively engage in its co-creation. The concept of 'lifelong learning' bridges archaic boundaries by distinguishing early career phases of intense knowledge acquisition (through formal 'learning') with subsequent knowledge utilisation (through professional practice or 'doing'). Set within this wider context, the growth in professional mobilities involving healthcare professionals will come as no surprise. In some cases, these mobilities may themselves represent 'migrations' as healthcare professionals identify opportunities for longer term relocation abroad (Buchan 2001). Recent years have seen a growing interest amongst British healthcare professionals in Australia and New Zealand contributing to what is often referred to, somewhat simplistically, as the 'brain drain' (Lumley 2011). In many other cases, mobilities take the form of shorter stays to gain exposure, respite or adventure in foreign climes (Hudson and Inkson 2006).

This book and the studies on which it is based focuses on one component of these complex mobility flows, namely temporary stays undertaken by National Health Service (NHS) employees in low- and middle-income countries (LMICs). The individuals and groups involved in these forms of movement are by no means homogenous, either in terms of personal characteristics or motivations (Bussell and Forbes 2002; Lewis 2006; Strachan 2009). The nature of their deployment, their roles in the receiving country and the objectives and quality of the placement organisation all vary enormously. Collectively, these forms of mobility are historically associated with voluntarism largely because the periods of time spent in the low-resource setting are not remunerated by the hosting organisation. (So, objectively, they are volunteers in the receiving country and organisation.) This does not mean that the individuals involved receive no financial support. The (quite contentious) concept of 'compensation' has been utilised to distinguish contributions to maintenance and travel and so on, from remuneration (as pay). In many respects, this tells us little about the motivations or roles of those involved and more about attempts to negotiate legal parameters on the part of deploying organisations.[1]

Whilst most 'volunteers' will not be remunerated as employees of the deploying or host organisation and therefore are technically unpaid (so 'volunteering'), the concept of 'volunteer' has various connotations and infers motivations associated with altruism. Many of the organisations involved in the deployment of NHS professionals and creating opportunities for these forms of mobility do have charitable objectives. The British Red Cross, for example, has been actively recruiting volunteers since the beginning of the Voluntary Aid Detachment Scheme, which deployed volunteers to treat wounded soldiers during the First World War. Fifty years later in 1958, Voluntary Services Overseas (VSO) began linking international volunteers to projects. There are now many smaller charities offering international volunteering placements, including the much-publicised response of volunteers to the Ebola crisis in West Africa. Altruism of one form or another, often linked to forms of religiosity, may stimulate interest in placements in low-resource settings but this is by no means the sole factor.

In reality it is extremely difficult to characterise any form of human mobility in terms of one or two key motivations. Migration (or mobility) decision-making almost always involves a complex range of interacting factors combining lifestyle with career and sometimes adventure or escape. And motivational factors may combine genuine free choice with increasing elements of what we have called the 'expectation of mobility' (Ackers and Gill 2008; Cox 2008), as early career mobility becomes a rite of passage shaping entry into highly prized careers such as medicine. In the context of gap year mobilities, Heath (2007) points to a rise in numbers and argues that the socio-demographic profile of those involved is changing because of the increasing cost of university education. The act of being mobile (irrespective of learning) and displaying that on CVs becomes an important means of 'gaining the edge' in the competition for entry to elite institutions and subsequent career progression. This form of CV-enhancement has become an increasing expectation amongst junior doctors and perhaps lies behind the remarkable growth in the percentage of doctors 'choosing' to work and travel after foundation year, which almost doubled from 2011 to 2013 (UKFPO 2013).

The emergence of the 'global health' concept and the connections it has forged between International Development and Health policies in the UK has added new dynamics and actors. The Tropical Health and Education Trust (THET) itself funded through UK Aid has actively sought to recruit 'volunteers' to support its Health Partnership Scheme

(HPS). Two of the authors of this book (Ackers and Ackers-Johnson) have managed the THET-funded Sustainable Volunteering Project (SVP)[2] which sought to harness volunteers in knowledge mobilisation projects in support of maternal and new-born health in Uganda. The SVP developed the concept of 'professional volunteer' in an attempt to capture the fact that the NHS staff deployed were first and foremost highly skilled professionals, and it was their knowledge and professionalism that were fostered and mobilised as much as any altruistic motivation. This conceptualisation of the people involved in international placements in low-resource settings as 'knowledge brokers' captures their roles perfectly but fails to engage with popular terminology. In our recent work in Uganda, we have tried to substitute the very loaded concept of 'volunteer' with the more familiar concept of 'international faculty' but this tends to work better for those individuals and organisations engaging with university actors. In this book, we have decided to stick with the concept of 'professional volunteer' (PV).

Recruiting PVs to knowledge mobilisation interventions involves a range of considerations. In reality recruiting and deploying organisations will be balancing the expressed needs (wants) of host organisations with the needs (and supply) of potential professional volunteers and a degree of 'tension' often exists between those demanding (seeking) professional volunteers and those supplying them. Hosting organisations will often articulate a need for very highly qualified and experienced faculty even privileging the more prestigious professions (such as surgery or obstetrics) over nursing, midwifery and allied health professions – and they will express a strong preference for long stays. Put simply, they are looking for knowledge rich 'teachers'. On the other hand, the supply of potential faculty available to deploying organisations is skewed in the direction of early career individuals often seeking shorter stays that fit within training programmes and life course decisions (Ackers 2015). These forms of shorter stay mobility of more junior cadres of staff may be what offer the greatest return to the NHS. From the perspective of the NHS then, they may be looking at exporting knowledge-hungry 'learners'. What is clear from our work is that this simple binary characterising teachers at one end of a continuum and 'learners' at the other fails entirely to capture the complexity of knowledge mobilisation and lifelong learning.

Notwithstanding the motivations behind the professional volunteering or the cadres involved, there is a general consensus in the literature that relevant and valuable learning happens as a result of this activity (Crisp

2014; Jones et al. 2013; Kiernan et al. 2014; Lumb and Murdoch-Eaton 2014). And, that learning is often described as 'transformational' or life-changing (Fee and Gray 2013). Banatvala and Macklow-Smith (1997) suggest that the experience doctors gain overseas contributes significantly towards their professional development and that their clinical, organisational and managerial skills are improved when they return to the UK. In practice, much of the existing research on professional voluntarism focuses on impacts on host settings (Ackers and Ackers-Johnson 2016) and undergraduate electives (Ahmed et al. 2016). To the extent that studies address the returns to professionals and their employing organisations, these often take the form of opinion pieces or small-scale case studies, with a significant emphasis on medical electives. Just as we know relatively little about the more specific learning outcomes associated with professional volunteering in general, we also need more detailed understanding of the contextual and organisational variables that facilitate or inhibit these different forms of learning.

Healthcare professionals on international placements will undertake a diverse range of activities reflecting the objectives and structure of the deploying agencies and projects. Some, especially if they are taking time out of their careers or towards the end of their careers, may actively select placements outside of formal health systems, in orphanages, religious or environmental projects (Bhatta et al. 2009). Whilst most early career professionals will seek out placements in healthcare settings, these will involve quite different organisational and professional settings to those they are accustomed to in the NHS. Disciplinary boundaries are often dissolved, and a doctor may find herself doing the work of a nurse and vice versa (Button and Green 2005; Longstaff 2012). They will often work at the boundaries of their specialities, undertaking activities they would not engage in in the UK, or working with different populations (Kiernan et al. 2014; Lumb and Murdoch-Eaton 2014). The objectives of the deploying organisations will also impact learning; placements focused on service delivery in humanitarian emergency relief work may play a bigger role in supporting explicit clinical skills than capacity-building projects such as the SVP with its focus on systems change and capacity-building. The level of supervision is also likely to shape learning in interesting and perhaps surprising ways. The emphasis on 'co-presence' in the SVP project (Ackers and Ackers-Johnson 2014) and resistance to lone working and gap-filling may enhance some forms of learning whilst potentially detracting from others.

## Supporting Career Mobility in Resource Constrained Environments: The UK NHS

The Global Financial Crisis and ensuing financial (austerity) constraints have adversely affected healthcare systems in most developed nations. In turn, this has put pressure on public healthcare systems to increase efficiency and reduce waste by adopting approaches used in private enterprise to promote 'lean healthcare'. There is growing concern that importing organisational systems from private companies may fail to achieve the goals of large public sector not-for-profit organisations. Gover et al. point to some of the potential barriers and political resistance to the imposition of 'lean' business models in public service environments and introduce a parallel concept of 'frugal innovation'. They define frugal innovation as the search for 'efficient, low costs solutions to everyday problems' capable of containing or reducing public healthcare spending, whilst simultaneously assuring levels of service and extending provision to marginalised groups. Frugal innovation, they suggest, demands a 'reconfiguration of capabilities, resources and competencies' (p. 3). Of central importance to this book, the concept of frugal or 'reverse' innovation (Zedtwitz et al. 2015) implies that low-resource settings characterised by stark resource constraints may stimulate relevant learning or knowledge mobilisation (Petrick and Juntiwasarakij 2011). Crisp captures this concept in his book *Turning the World Upside Down: The search for global health in the 21st century*. Put simply, he argues that his book, 'explores what richer countries can learn from poorer ones' through processes of co-development. Whilst frugal innovation is often described by reference to physical devices such as low cost, 'no-frills' equipment or prosthetics, the concept also extends in interesting ways to aspects of human resource management such as 'task-shifting'[3] (Schneeberger and Mathai 2015).

The UK National Health Service, as a universal service providing free healthcare at the point of use, and in the context of increasing dependency and medical advances, inevitably faces ongoing funding challenges. It is in this specific context that the case for expanding resource on professional mobility needs to be fully justified to NHS managers, employees and patients. Increasing numbers of NHS providers are in financial difficulties. In 2011–12 only 24% of NHS Trusts[4] reported overspending (The Kings Fund 2015). The projected figures for the end of 2016 suggest it is likely to be in the region of 67%, with 89% of acute hospitals projecting a deficit

(Appleby et al. 2016). For the first time since the Kings Trust Quarterly Monthly Report began in 2011, more than half of the trust directors believe that the quality of care in their local area has worsened in the past year (Appleby et al. 2016).

The NHS financial crisis is progressively worsening despite government initiatives to reduce spending (Appleby et al. 2016), and it would seem that human resource deficits lie at the heart of the current funding crisis. Addicott et al. (2015), for example, argue that 70% of costs incurred by NHS trusts are workforce related. This human resource crisis has left NHS managers increasingly reliant on a very expensive locum or agency staff. Figures suggest that 80% of hospital trusts spend more than £1,000 per shift on medical cover for doctors. This equates to more than £2 billion in two years, which could have paid the wages of 48,000 nurses or 33,000 junior doctors over the same period (Donnelly and Mulhern 2012). Migration trends lie at the heart of the problem, and the potential solution. In order to fill the vacancies, 69% of trusts are actively recruiting doctors and nurses from overseas (Hughes and Clarke 2016); 11% of NHS staff and 26% of doctors are non-British (Sidduique 2014). Professional migration is not unidirectional; the number of doctors seeking to emigrate from the UK has increased by 20% in the past five years (Boffey 2014).

The pressure on human resource budgets is also manifest in demands for workforce efficiency and productivity; the NHS requires more from current staff than ever before, resulting in an emphasis on resourcefulness, cost efficiency, flexibility and inter-professional working (Health Education England 2016a; 2016b).

These demands for improved productivity imply further investment in staff through continuing professional development (CPD). Health Education England (HEE) has organisational responsibility for the commissioning of training and the professional development of NHS professionals. It aims 'to support the delivery of excellent healthcare and health improvement to the patients and public of England by ensuring that the workforce of today and tomorrow has the right numbers, skills, values and behaviours, at the right time and in the right place' (Health Education England 2016C).

Health Education England's 15-year Strategic Plan focuses on the skills and competencies needed for the future workforce (HEE 2014). The emergence of new infections and antimicrobial resistances underlines an emphasis on cross-professional training to support generic competencies. The plan is based on core characteristics of the future workforce and includes the need for adaptable skills that are responsive to evidence and innovation. It also proposes that finite resources need to be invested more wisely and healthcare facilities should focus on coordinated care delivered by multidisciplinary teams. The NHS 5 *year Forward View* is a similar, more short-term, focused document outlining what the NHS plans to achieve in the next five years (NHS England 2014). It also places an emphasis on training to equip staff with skills and flexibilities to deliver new models of care with a focus on innovation and an investment in improving leadership.

In this environment, it is hardly surprising that many NHS employers are reluctant to agree to requests for leave to undertake international placements even when they involve a high level of self-funding. 'Back-fill' (funding staff to cover the work of those who are not on duty) represents a major and very expensive challenge to line managers on the ground (Longstaff 2012). And, in the current environment back-fill will often have to be provided by agency or locum staff who are in turn significantly more expensive (Donnelly and Mulhern 2012). Smith et al. (2012) suggest that this situation leads to reluctance to release staff for international placements.

In addition to political and economic pressures on NHS budgets, government spending on International Development has also been called into question. In reality, the UK Aid budget has been successfully ring-fenced and insulated from public sector cuts. However, this has come with increasing pressure for public accountability reflected in an explicit policy emphasis on the UK 'national interest' (UK Aid 2015). In future, all spending on aid will have to demonstrate that it either responds to a direct threat to British interests (such as terrorism or climate change) or has spill-over components that present a simultaneous challenge to the UK; global health features in this group with specific reference to epidemics and anti-microbial resistance. Whilst there is no specific reference in this chapter to professional volunteering amongst NHS employees, the case remains to be made that this form of UK investment falls squarely in the 'national interest'. Crisp (2010) suggests that in the brave new world of global health we are all increasingly connected and interdependent. It is not only health systems in low-resource settings that are challenged by issues of sustainability and funding, but high-resource settings now face the same problems, and so the growing mobility of the international labour force plays a key role in the mutual cross-fertilisation of knowledge and ideas.

To summarise, the UK NHS faces a serious human resource crisis; this is manifest in two ways of direct relevance to our research. In the first instance, we are dealing with an immediate shortage of staff. In this context, international placements represent an additional and immediate burden on the already pressed systems. Secondly, the pressure for efficiency and productivity increasingly places an emphasis on improved continuing professional development, and in this context, international placements present potentially fruitful and highly efficient opportunities for lesson learning and 'frugal innovation'.

Whilst there is strong evidence to support the view that international placements present valuable and enjoyable opportunities for healthcare professionals, there is insufficient evidence at the present to justify and lend public credibility to NHS expenditure in this area of activity. The quality of the learning and potential for effective knowledge mobilisation and innovation requires a higher level of specification aligning, wherever possible, to identified staff development priorities and costing accordingly. Every international placement is distinct in terms of its context, the activities that the professional volunteer engages in, and the learning opportunities that they present. We need to understand more about the conditions under which mutual learning is optimised and opportunities for translational impact (for the NHS) generated. What exactly this learning entails and how it is facilitated within an international context or how it maps onto CPD needs in the NHS is less well known (Jones et al. 2013).

What interests us in this book and the *Measuring the Outcomes of Volunteering for Education* (MOVE) study[5] is the collective impact of these disparate processes on the National Health Service as an employer with responsibility for the delivery of universal public healthcare in the UK.

The MOVE study was a collaborative project conducted by the research teams based at the School of Nursing, Midwifery, Social Work & Social Sciences, University of Salford and Manchester University Medical School. It ran for two years from 2014 until 2016 and was commissioned and funded by Health Education England (Department of Health). The key objectives were as follows:

## Objectives

1. What forms of mobility are present within the current NHS workforce?
2. What forms of knowledge are effectively mobilised during these mobility episodes?

3. How does knowledge gain map onto strategic training objectives in the NHS? (How relevant is the knowledge?)
4. What organisational and contextual variables facilitate the optimal acquisition of these forms of knowledge?
5. What barriers exist to international placements and to the mobilisation of the knowledge gained from them on return to the NHS (is the NHS receptive to new knowledge?)
6. Can the evidence base derived from this research support the development of a psychometric tool capable of measuring quantitatively the outcomes associated with professional volunteering in LMICs?

## THE MOVE STUDY: METHODS

The MOVE study built on extensive previous action-research on professional voluntarism within the frame of the THET-funded Sustainable Volunteering Project (SVP). Further details of this are contained in Appendix 2 and reported on in Ackers et al. (2016) and Ackers and Ackers-Johnson (2016). Building on many years' experience of research on highly skilled mobilities and knowledge transfer processes, the evaluation strategy included a range of methods complementing and balancing each other through a process of triangulation. The study adopted a multi-method approach designed to capture as accurately as possible the complexity of learning that takes place during international placements. We utilised the following data sources:

- A review of available research and literature on professional volunteering.[6]
- A face-to-face electronic survey of staff in a selection of NHS facilities in the North West of England.
- Semi-structured interviews with key informants and returned professional volunteers (both within the frame of the SVP ($n = 150^7$) and drawing on the survey population ($n = 51$))
- Analysis of documentary evidence collated as part of the SVP including volunteers' monthly reports
- Ethnographic observation and fieldwork with professional volunteers deployed via the SVP to Uganda.

In addition to this, members of the MOVE team (headed by Dr. Byrne-Davis) have utilised a Delphi approach for assessing the possibility of developing a psychometric tool to measure the core outcomes associated with professional volunteering. The tool is not reported in this book.

## NOTES

1. For details see https://www.gov.uk/volunteering/pay-and-expenses
2. A summary of the SVP is contained in Appendix 2.
3. Defined as the 'systematic delegation of tasks to less-specialised cadres' or 'optimising health worker roles'.
4. A National Health Service trust is an organisation within the English NHS generally serving either a geographical area or a specialised function (such as an ambulance service). In any particular location, there may be several trusts involved in the different aspects of healthcare for a resident.
5. Companion volumes focus on the impact on the host (LMIC) settings (Ackers et al. 2016) and undergraduate mobilities (Ackers et al. 2016).
6. This included a systematic review undertaken by Tyler and explained in detail in her doctoral thesis (unpublished).
7. The numbers cited here are constantly increasing as we continue to deploy volunteers and assess impacts.

# CHAPTER 2

# Internationalisation and Placement Activity in the UK National Health Service

**Abstract** This chapter presents and discusses the findings from a survey conducted in the North West of England designed to gauge overall patterns of international exposure amongst all cadres of staff in the UK's National Health Service.

**Keywords** Internationalisation · Overseas placements · Current usage levels (in NHS)

## INTRODUCTION

Very little is known about the prevalence of international exposure across the NHS. In contrast to the highly accurate and detailed NHS workforce summaries which are available from central government sources, information specifically concerned with professional volunteering placements is often piecemeal and deals only with discrete settings or departments. Organisations responsible for volunteer deployments, such as Voluntary Service Overseas or the Tropical Health and Education Trust, have conducted some small-scale surveys of their own volunteers, but this gives little impression of the overall propensity to engage in international placements and may give the impression that the phenomenon is far more common than it really is.

We thought it would be useful to contextualise the findings on learning outcomes derived from the qualitative interviews with professional

© The Author(s) 2017
H.L. Ackers et al., *Healthcare, Frugal Innovation, and Professional Voluntarism*, DOI 10.1007/978-3-319-48366-5_2

volunteers within an overall understanding of prevalence and patterns of this form of mobility. Chapter 1 raised concerns about the growing expectation of mobility in healthcare professions. It also positioned the study in the context of the evolving skills agenda in the NHS and the emphasis on soft skills and multidisciplinary team working. Both of these issues raise the issue of inclusivity and the importance of opening up opportunities for all staff across cadres and over the life course. Chapter 1 also raised concerns about the financial implications that these forms of mobility generate in terms of providing staff cover. The survey findings provide an important context for these discussions.

## THE NHS STAFF SURVEY

Survey research is often hampered by non-response skewing findings. (See, for example, Bhatta 2009; Baruch Y and Holtom 2008; Evans and Mathur 2005; Barclay et al. 2002.) We anticipated a greater response rate to an online survey from those staff who had experienced international placements than those who had not. Pilot work supported this assertion as staff in technical areas or laboratory work who had not experienced international mobility immediately interpreted the survey, despite assurances, as implying that they were not eligible to respond. We were particularly keen to sample a wide range of staff, including those whom we may expect to have had less opportunity to engage in international placements. With this objective in mind we decided not to opt for a blanket email/online survey but rather to attempt to gather results on a face-to-face basis to optimise completion rates.

Attempting to sample the whole population of (1.3 million) NHS employees could only have been achieved with great difficulty and probably only through an online survey tool administrated via Trusts. Our relationships with institutions in the North West enabled us to target a subpopulation that we consider to be broadly representative of the wider NHS. We therefore decided to focus our recruitment on a small number of hospitals and community medical centres within a single NHS region in the North West of England. These included two large regional teaching hospitals: Salford Royal Infirmary, Salford, and Wythenshawe Hospital (the University Hospital of South Manchester NHS Foundation Trust). We also undertook recruitment at Liverpool Women's Hospital, which is a major obstetrics, gynaecology and neonatology research hospital; and Liverpool Community Health Trust, which is a large regional hub for the administration of over 3000 NHS staff in the North West. Data from these institutions were supplemented with findings gathered from the

2015 Royal College of Nursing Research Conference, and a large Community-Based Medical Education training event held in April 2015. Following a successful pilot survey conducted at Liverpool Women's Hospital, we decided it would be most effective to target our activity on busy public areas within each site, such as main entrances, cafeterias and arterial thoroughfares. We reasoned that such areas would be used by the whole range of hospital employees, and there would be the best chance of accessing a broad sample. The research team worked in groups of three or four, identifying potential respondents as those with NHS identification badges. At the Wythenshawe site, we were also able to attend three large staff orientation events organised by the hospital's HR department. These events, which were essentially held to welcome new starters at the hospital, attracted a wide range of people from different staff groups.

The survey was designed to be conducted on a one-to-one basis by researchers using an iPad running *eForms* software (University of Manchester 2015). It was deliberately framed to be very quick to complete – around two minutes – and was anonymous. Using *eForms* streamlined the process of participant engagement and meant that the survey could be conducted wholly electronically. Once a member of staff had been approached and agreed to take part, they were given the iPad and worked through the various simple sections of the survey (see below). Respondents were automatically assigned a code number by the *eForms* system, and their anonymous responses were stored offline on the iPad. Data were downloaded to a central online database at the end of each fieldwork session. Field work was conducted in the various settings between January and August 2015. The survey consisted of seven sections.

## CADRE

The categorisations we listed were derived from eight standard employment cadres currently utilised by human resource departments across the NHS:

1. Allied health professionals
2. Healthcare scientists
3. Medical and dental
4. NHS infrastructure
5. Scientific and technical
6. Ambulance staff
7. Nursing midwifery and health visitors
8. Clinical support staff

## CAREER STAGE

1. Pre-university
2. Student
3. Early-career
4. Mid-career
5. Experienced /senior
6. Post retirement

Subsequent sections were related to age, gender and nationality. Those who indicated that they had spent time in another country, either as an employee or volunteer, proceeded to a final section (6), which focused on specific details for each time of stay abroad. This section included questions on the economic status of the country (high, middle or low income), and the career stage they were at when abroad: *pre-university; student; early-career; mid-career; experienced /senior; post retirement*. We also collected basic qualitative information at this point relating to length of stay and the type of placement if this was relevant. At the conclusion of the survey respondents who indicated that they would like to be sent information on the outcome of the study were asked to share an email address or phone number. A copy of the survey is given in Appendix 2.

## RESULTS

SPSS software was used to provide basic descriptive statistics and isolate the key features of the data. Overall, a total of 911 NHS employees completed the survey.

### Sample Characteristics

Table 2.1 shows the relative proportions of different staff cadres currently employed in the NHS as a whole (column **A**), along with the relative percentages of staff specifically employed in the North-West region where the staff survey was conducted (NHS-ESR 2013) (column **B**). Column **C** shows the proportion of respondents from different staff groups who actually took part in the survey. Column **D** gives the proportion of staff by cadre who were interviewed for the qualitative arm of the MOVE study.

It can be seen that in line with our broad hypothesis, the relative *proportion* of staff that go to make up the NHS workforce nationally

**Table 2.1** The survey population compared to the NHS workforce and interview sample

| Staff group | (A) Relative percentages of staff in the total NHS workforce (%) | (B) Relative percentages of staff in the North West region. (NHS-ESR 2013) (%) | (C) Survey respondents (%) | (D) Interviewees (%) |
|---|---|---|---|---|
| Nurse/ midwife/ health visitor | 30 | 31 | 31 | 32 |
| Allied health professionals | 8 | 6 | 14 | 13 |
| Medical and dental | 10 | 10 | 32 | 35 |
| Clinical support staff | 29 | 27 | 10 | 4 |
| NHS infrastructure | 16 | 20 | 7 | 14 |
| Ambulance staff | 2 | 2 | 2 | 0 |
| Health scientist | 5 | 4 | 4 | 2 |

*Source*: Created by the authors.

(column **A**) is very closely matched to the proportion of staff employed in the North-West Region (column **B**). This supports our contention that the survey data obtained in the context of a single region could be reasonably expected to reflect the situation across the entire organisation – at least in relation to the kind of non-regionally specific issues we are concerned with. The only staff cadre with any significant variation between regional and national levels is *infrastructure*, and even with this group, there is only a 4% difference. The slightly higher proportion of infrastructure staff relative to the national figure may be due to a variety of factors but is likely to reflect the particular organisation and management idiosyncrasies which have evolved in the North West. In the context of this survey (and indeed the wider MOVE project), these kinds of variation are unlikely to have a significant impact. Although our sampling process was largely opportunistic (see above), the sampling process achieved the level of diversity that we had planned for (column **C**). Significantly, the percentage of *nurse /midwife /health visitor* staff we engaged with accurately reflects both the national and regional figures. However, *medical and dental* were over-represented and clinical support staff and infrastructure staff were underrepresented.

### International Placements

Table 2.2 provides the relative percentages of staff from the various cadres who had engaged in overseas activity at some stage in their educational career. It can be seen that overall, 42% of those in our survey (389) reported at least one overseas placement experience.

The three highest responding groups were medical and dental with 140 respondents (36%); nursing/midwifery and health visitor (21%); and allied health professionals (18%). The remaining groups were composed of clinical support staff (15%); NHS infrastructure (4%); health scientists (4%); and ambulance staff (2%)

It is no great surprise that in line with the focus of much of the literature on volunteering and placements within health and medical contexts the highest proportion of staff with overseas experience were *medical and dental* (see, for example, BMA 2009; RCN 2010). This is likely to be a reflection of the way in which medical training in the UK has traditionally valued the experience that students gain from time abroad. The option is to participate in an overseas placement often being built into, or at least available through UK-based clinical training programmes (Gedde et al. 2011; Tooke 2009).

It is significant in the context of current policy initiatives that, although the next most populous group in terms of placement activity were *nurses, midwives and health visitors* (21.1% of volunteers), the

Table 2.2   Volunteering experiences by cadre

| Professional group | Proportion of sample |
|---|---|
| Nurse/midwife/health visitor | (21%) 82 |
| Allied healthcare professionals | (18%) 71 |
| Medical and dental | (36%) 140 |
| Support to clinical staff | (15%) 58 |
| NHS infrastructure | (4%) 15 |
| Ambulance staff | (2%) 8 |
| Health scientist | (4%) 5 |
| **Total** | 389 |

*Source*: Created by the authors.

third group, *allied health professionals*, was of a similar size (18.3%). This group as a whole has not traditionally engaged in overseas activity as part of NHS-based training, although particular sub-groups including physiotherapists and speech and language therapists do have a more active tradition of incorporating international placements and training (Rodger et al. 2008). The relatively high percentage of staff in this group as a whole may indicate that there are a large number of individuals who have managed to navigate their way through the process of organising and undertaking an overseas outing within the demands of their everyday roles, and not necessarily with the structural support enjoyed by some of their colleagues. The detailed makeup of such a group would be usefully analysed in further work, as they will have a first-hand experience of just where systemic and organisational barriers can develop.

It is interesting to reflect on the perceptions of one survey respondent (a theatre technician) who had not experienced an international placement himself but had views about their relative contribution to learning:

> It doesn't seem to be offered to people [theatre assistants] in the operating theatres cos we're on the coal face doing the important work [laughs]... Value? Possibly, possibly not. I'd love to go abroad and see how other people work but value – possibly not. I've spoken to people who've gone abroad and they've come back and they don't seem to bring very much back with them to be quite honest. They tell you how – people who have been to Africa, for example, or India – they come back and they say it's been great for them to help, to see how other people work. But the only thing they seem to bring back is that they're really happy to be back and they're not working in those conditions anymore. You know, the NHS, seems to be a good place to work really and they realise that when they come back and they see how the rest of the world works.

### Placement Location

Table 2.3 shows the broad socio-economic status of the countries where staff reported having gained overseas experience. 20% (77) had worked in a high-income location; 22% (86) in a middle-income location; and 58% (226) in a low-income location.

Over half of the respondents reported an experience in a low-resource setting. The clear tendency for professional volunteering to be focused on low-income locations such as sub-Saharan Africa and India is borne out in

**Table 2.3**  Economic status of locations where staff reported overseas experience

| Location | % of staff |
| --- | --- |
| High-income | 20 |
| Middle-income | 22 |
| Low-income | 58 |

*Source*: Created by the authors.

the literature. As early as the late 1980s Graitcer et al. (1989) were suggesting that 100,000 non-governmental sponsored volunteers worked in developing countries, with much smaller numbers choosing to go to more wealthy locations. More recent estimates by the Department of Health have supported this (Department of Health 2010a), and at a broader corporate level, a recent survey by internet placement brokers *Go Overseas* noted that the top five most searched-for locations for voluntary work and placement opportunities in 2014 were the Philippines, Thailand, India, Nepal and Cambodia (Go Overseas 2014). Interestingly, the Philippines headed the list at the time of their survey due to people specifically wishing to help with the response to typhoon Haiyan, which struck the area in late 2013. From a more functional perspective Bhatta et al. (2009) have outlined how the tendency for low-income locations to be favoured over high-income ones can also be influenced by placement providers. Well-established organisations such as VSO concentrate their efforts exclusively on low-income areas, and contextually too, the idea of 'overseas volunteering' is rarely associated with locations such as America or Western Europe unless the activities undertaken are concerned with low-income or deprived sectors. Volunteering in high-income settings can evoke a slightly different kind of motivations, and there can be a shift from the purely altruistic to something with a more personal focus; activities, while still essentially 'voluntary', can become labelled more as internships, with a more overt focus on work experience and career development.

## *Gender*

The overall sample included more females than males (519 females compared to 392 males). This echoes the gender balance in the NHS. A recent report by the National Health Service Employers (NHSE 2016) indicates that around 77% NHS employees are female. Figures from NHS Digital (NHSD 2016) note that it is only in the cadre represented by ambulance staff that male employees predominate (62% are male).

Our sample indicated that 217 females and 172 males had voluntary or overseas experience. Table 2.4 shows the overall gender balance among volunteers across the different staff grades.

In terms of females, nurses, midwives and health visitors reported the most experience of international placements (34%), followed by medical/dental (27%). Amongst males, medical/dental cadres represented the largest group; (48%), followed by Allied Health Professionals (25%) (Table 2.5).

Within the individual staff group, it can be seen that the balance between male and female volunteers broadly reflects the gender balance

**Table 2.4**  Overall proportion of staff by gender volunteering in another country

| Professional group | Female | Male | Totals (M &FM) |
|---|---|---|---|
| Nurse/midwife/health visitor | 34% (74) | 5% (8) | 82 |
| Medical and dental | 27% (58) | 48% (82) | 140 |
| Support to clinical staff | 17% (38) | 11% (20) | 58 |
| NHS infrastructure | 6% (13) | 1% (2) | 15 |
| Health scientist | 2% (5) | 6% (10) | 15 |
| Allied healthcare professionals | 1% (28) | 25% (43) | 71 |
| Ambulance staff | 1% (1) | 4% (7) | 8 |
| Totals | 100%/217 | 100%/172 | 389 |

Source: Created by the authors.

**Table 2.5**  Gender breakdown by cadre (international volunteering)

| Professional group | Female | Male | Total (M & FM) |
|---|---|---|---|
| Nurse/midwife/health visitor | 90% (74) | 10% (8) | 82 |
| NHS infrastructure | 87% (13) | 13% (2) | 15 |
| Support to clinical staff | 66% (38) | 34% (20) | 58 |
| Medical and dental | 41% (58) | 59% (82) | 140 |
| Allied healthcare professionals | 40% (28) | 60% (43) | 71 |
| Health scientist | 34% (5) | 66% (10) | 15 |
| Ambulance staff | 12% (1) | 88% (7) | 8 |
| Total | 217 | 172 | 389 |

Source: Created by the authors.

of the overall NHS workforce (National Health Service England 2014). The heavy bias towards females in the organisation as a whole is matched by the predominance of female volunteers in most staff cadres. For example, only 10% of nurses, midwives and health visitors in the NHS are male (NHS 2016), and this proportion is reproduced in our volunteer sample – 10% of male nurses and midwives had volunteered or worked overseas. Similarly, the overall proportions of male and female doctors in the NHS are currently relatively balanced, with 55% male and 45% female (National Health Service 2016). Our sample revealed that the numbers of male and female volunteers in this cadre also broadly followed this trend (59% male and 41% female). What this appears to suggest is that the predominance of female healthcare workers noted in many locations may be due more to the fact that there are proportionately more women working in this field (e.g. nurses). It is not that women per se are more inclined to become involved, or that it is seen as a particularly 'female' activity (Fig. 2.1).

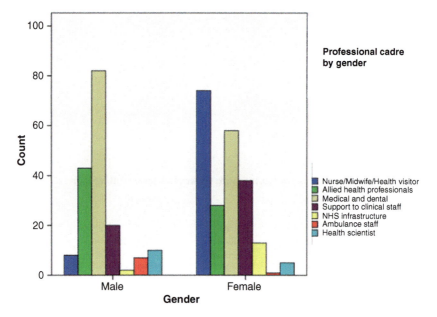

**Fig. 2.1** Professional cadre by gender

*Source*: Created by the authors.

## Nationality

Although nationality data for the NHS workforce is officially collected (NHS digital 2016), it is currently categorised by the country of origin, rather than under the socio-demographic headings we required (i.e. *British, European, Non-EU National*). We derived approximate equivalent proportions by manually assigning the 212 countries in the official workforce data to our nationality categories. We acknowledge that this is only likely to give a broad approximation of current levels as there is a degree of ambiguity over where many locations might be categorised, and further bias will be introduced by the high number of staff who are officially listed as 'nationality unknown' (22%). However, even with these caveats, the proportion of staff in our survey sample (column **B**, Table 2.6) does appear to reflect the levels found in the workforce overall (column **A**, Table 2.6). The major difference is the number of Europeans listed. Staff from European countries accounted for around 2% of the total NHS workforce, whereas our sample included just over 12%. Given that it is limited to a single category, this difference may reflect local socio-demographic conditions and is also likely to be influenced by the significant number of 'unknowns' (22%) in the national data. Significantly, the proportion of staff in our sample who had volunteered (column **C**, Table 2.6/Fig. 2.2) is closely matched by the makeup of the entire sample (column **B**, Table 2.6). This appears to indicate that in the healthcare sector the propensity to volunteer or work overseas is not dependent on country of origin.

**Table 2.6** Nationality of NHS staff and survey respondents compared

| Nationality | (A) Approximate proportion of NHS workforce* | (B) Proportion of overall sample | (C) Proportion of staff who had volunteered |
|---|---|---|---|
| British | (70%) 850000 | (80.6%) 734 | (78.4 %) 305 |
| European | (2%) 24500 | (11.7%) 107 | (12.1%) 47 |
| Non-EU national (developing country) | (5%) 62000 | (6.5%) 59 | (6.7%) 26 |
| Non-EU national (developed country) | (1%) 9000 | (1.1%) 10 | (2.6%) 10 |
| Other/unknown | (22%) 264000 | (0.1%) 1 | (0.3) 1 |
| Total | 1.2 M | 911 | 389 |

*Source*: Created by the authors.

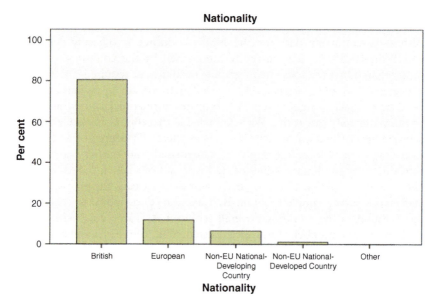

**Fig. 2.2**    Proportion of surveyed staff who had volunteered (column C)

*Source*: Created by the authors.

## Career Stage

Table 2.7 illustrates the gender split within the survey, cross-tabulated by career stage. It can be seen that most males took an international placement while they were students (33% of male volunteers) followed by early career (26%) and mid-career (22%). The remaining 19% were split between pre-university (6%), experienced (11%) and post-retirement (2%). Women also tended to favour international placements while they were students (41%), with 31% going during their early career, and 14% at mid-career stage (Fig. 2.3):

Overall then, the survey indicated that the majority of overseas work or volunteering activity takes place during the early stages of people's careers, particularly during *student* and *early career* phases. For clinical staff, who may to some extent have opportunities to do this kind of activity built into their training, this is to be expected. For other staff cadres too, the period during which people traditionally have more freedom (i.e. time removed from the inevitable build-up of commitments such as starting a family) to

**Table 2.7** Career stage while working or volunteering in another country

| Career stage while abroad | Male | Female |
|---|---|---|
| Pre-university | (6%) 11 | (6%) 13 |
| Student | (33%) 56 | (41%) 88 |
| Early career | (26%) 46 | (31%) 68 |
| Mid-career | (22% )38 | (14%) 31 |
| Experienced | (11%) 18 | (7%) 15 |
| Post-retirement | (2%) 3 | (1%) 2 |
| **Totals** | 172 | 217 |

*Source*: Created by the authors.

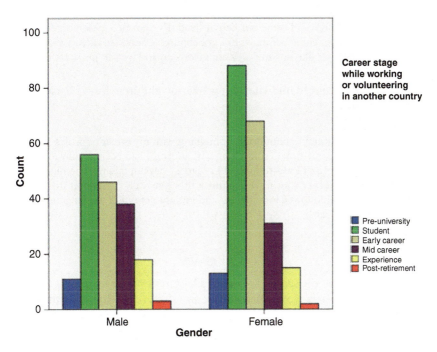

**Fig. 2.3**  Career stage while working or volunteering in another country

*Source*: Created by the authors.

engage with a spell abroad often coincides with these early career stages. Of course, not all staff follow the conventional route straight from education into training, and whereas this direct path may be the norm for medics, for other cadres, the process can be much more circuitous. Many people come to nursing, for example, after working in other careers for a period, and this obviously has implications in terms of how they may be able to deal with their other commitments. Others, like some of the midwives we interviewed for the qualitative strand of the study, had reached a point in their careers where their personal commitments had lessened and they were able to consider some time away. Kelly told us:

> I'd been a midwife for a long time and I wanted a year out. So I applied to join VSO and got in. I was just doing all that sort of stuff and then I saw [a project in Uganda] so I came out here instead. I've got two grown up boys. I think you either come before you've got children/family, so there's a lot of young people. Or like me, our kids are grown up and we can just walk out.

Sandra, an experienced midwife with grown-up children, found herself in a similar position:

> I have always thought about doing something with my career or profession. Take some time out and do something with it. And I had been a midwife for a very long time, and I was thinking I have to do development, something in developing countries with it. It was just a thought really. I thought if I did this, my CV would look a lot different and I might get out of working nights and delivering babies.

### *Length of Stay*

For the purpose of the survey, we defined length of stay as *short-term* (under a week); *medium-term* (over two weeks); *long-term* (over three months) and *extended* or *settlement* (over one year). On average, the most popular length of stay for an overseas placement or voluntary work was *medium-term*, with 50% of respondents indicating that they stayed for up to three months.

It was much less usual for staff to report stays of over one year; only 8% indicated that they had been away for over a year. In terms of the gender breakdown, males tended to favour medium-term placements (46%) followed by long-term stays (24%). Eighteen per cent of males reported a short-term stay. In comparison, just over half (52%) females took a

**Table 2.8** Length of placement stay by gender

| Length of time abroad | Male | Female | Overall proportion (M and FM) |
|---|---|---|---|
| Short term | (18%) 31 | (15%) 33 | (16%) 64 |
| Medium term | (46%) 80 | (52%) 114 | (50%) 194 |
| Long term | (24%) 41 | (19%) 42 | (21%) 83 |
| Extended | (8%) 13 | (9%) 18 | (8%) 31 |
| Other | (4%) 7 | (5%) 10 | (5%) 17 |
| **Totals** | 172 | 217 | 389 |

*Source*: Created by the authors.

medium-term placement; 19%, a long-term and 15%, a short-term placement. Respondents who chose to make an extended stay were similarly matched in terms of gender: 8% were male and 9% were female. Overall, gender does not appear to have a great deal of impact on length of stay. The proportion of males and females in each time frame closely matches the percentages in the overall sample (Table 2.8).

## *Age Group and Length of Stay*

Table 2.9 and Fig. 2.4 provide the age group of staff cross-tabulated against length of stay. It can be seen that the majority of respondents engaged in international placement were from the age group 'below 25' to '41–50', which equates to 288 out of a total of 389 respondents (74%). 94 respondents, or 50%, engaged in medium-term placements. Overall, medium-term placements were the most popular, with a total of 49% of respondents across all age groups. Settlement/extended stays represented the smallest discrete group, with 8% respondents.

In many ways, the data relating to the age groups within which staff routinely fall when they work abroad appear to reflect socio-demographic conventions. The majority of staff with overseas experience, for example, come from the below 25 age group, and those who were 41–50. Almost half of these (49.9%) reported taking a medium-term placement. Medium-term placements were defined as over two weeks, but less than three months, and as such represent a period away which may be incorporated into the ongoing training and employment, without necessarily causing too much disruption. It is also a time frame that meshes conveniently with commercially available, medically focused, student placement schemes. In fact, many such schemes are clearly market driven and are designed to be

**Table 2.9**   Length of stay by age group

| Age group | Short term | Medium term | Long term | Extended | Other |
|---|---|---|---|---|---|
| Below 25 | (22%) 14 | (21%) 41 | (11%) 9 | (10%) 3 | (12%) 2 |
| 26–30 | (8%) 5 | (10%) 19 | (12%) 10 | (3%) 1 | (17%) 3 |
| 31–40 | (17%) 11 | (23%) 44 | (22%) 18 | (29%) 9 | (29%) 5 |
| 41–50 | (25%) 16 | (18%) 36 | (31%) 26 | (35%) 11 | (30%) 5 |
| 51–60 | (9%) 6 | (11%) 22 | (11%) 9 | (13%) 4 | (0%) 0 |
| 61–70 | (14%) 9 | (14%) 27 | (9%) 8 | (10%) 3 | (12%) 2 |
| 71+ | (5%) 3 | (3%) 5 | (4%) 3 | (0%) 0 | (0%) 0 |
| Totals | 64 | 194 | 83 | 31 | 17 |

*Source*: Created by the authors.

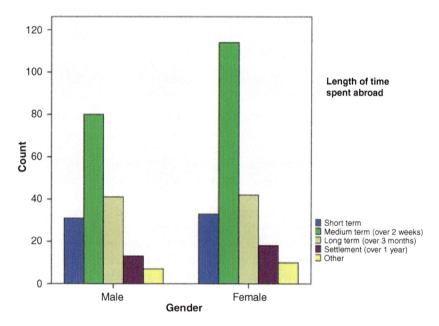

**Fig. 2.4**   Length of time abroad

*Source*: Created by the authors.

as attractive as possible to their potential customers. In terms of cadres, for example, it tends to be doctors who are able to take longer periods abroad. However, as this anaesthetist told us, the pathway to taking a placement is not always straightforward, even for this group:

> I wanted to do volunteering for a long time. I wanted to do it in an early stage of my life but I never quite did it, and although the GMC and the Royal College of Anaesthetists, and the various bodies say yeah, we support volunteering, we support working in developing countries, my individual deanery, my individual school was dead-set against it. I think they've been dead-set against it for about two years. So now I've been trying to build it in to a training placement by taking time out unrecognised for training. I've just been hitting brick walls to a point where they just kept on changing the goal posts. This is something I've got an email chain about going back about two years. When I actually asked them about wanting to do something like this, I got so frustrated that I ended up just making a decision to do my own thing. I did have a volunteer placement in Ethiopia. So I resigned my NHS job because I felt so disenfranchised and I thought well if I don't do it now, then when am I going to do it? I can always re-join registrar training, I can always get my accreditation another way.

### Multiple Placement Experience

In our sample, multiple placement experiences tended to be relatively unusual. Only 10 respondents reported three periods of overseas activity, and only six of those with overseas experience reported four. All of those with multiple placement experiences came from the three staff groups incorporating *midwife /nurse /health visitor* (3 with 3 placements, and 3 with 4 placements); *allied HCP* (2 with 3 placements and 1 with 4 placements), and *medical and dental* (5 with 3 placements and 2 with 4 placements), respectively.

The issue of staff who engage in multiple placements, or periods of voluntary work abroad, is revealing. Again, in our sample, it was the *medical and dental, nursing*, and *allied healthcare professional* cadres where activity was focused. None of the other staff groupings were represented. This skewing of multiple placements towards these groups – and by extension, the employment and socio-demographic conditions which underpin them – may again be a reflection of the way in which medical training and career structuring within the NHS allow these cadres the freedom to engage in such activity.

## SUMMARY

In this chapter, we have outlined the findings from our NHS staff volunteering and overseas placement survey. This formed a discrete component of the MOVE study. The survey was primarily intended to capture a snapshot of current levels of volunteering and overseas placement activity across NHS staff grades in the North West, and we would argue that we achieved this. We are also confident that our broader aim of being able to use our findings to give a rough indication of the position across the whole of the NHS has been fulfilled. Like any large national organisation, the NHS is fairly homogenous in terms of the way its local structures are organised. The relative staffing levels we were able to capture are therefore likely to be reproduced across the organisation as a whole. By extension, levels of volunteering and overseas placement activity amongst these staff at a regional level are likely to be reproduced nationally. In the context of the NHS, it has traditionally been trainee doctors who were most likely to engage with a period of work, or placement overseas, and our survey reflects this trend. Nurses and midwives too have more recently begun to take advantage of slightly more flexible employment arrangements which have given them easier access to such placements within their career structure, and this is also reflected in our sample. In line with established NHS management and training models, our survey showed that although some degree of overseas placement activity is undertaken by a relatively high proportion of NHS staff, such activity is heavily skewed towards higher clinical staff grades. However, significant numbers of allied health professionals and equivalent non-clinical cadres also report overseas experience, and if current initiatives gain momentum, we would anticipate that these numbers will continue to rise.

# What Do Health Workers Learn on International Placements?

**Abstract** Chapter 3 reviews existing research and the findings from qualitative interviews with returned professional volunteers to identify core learning outcomes associated with International Placements.

**Keywords** Learning outcomes · Interviews · Continuing professional development (CPD)

## INTRODUCTION

Drawing on the literature reviewed and our qualitative work with returned professional volunteers, Chapter 3 summarises what is known about the forms of learning that can take place on international placements. It is extremely difficult to isolate or specify key skills or competences gained from professional voluntarism. First, the phenomenon is itself incredibly broad encompassing an overwhelming diversity of experience and learning across professional cadres and career stages. Secondly, the most common response when interviewing returned volunteers about placement learning is for them to refer to the transformational or life-changing impact it has had. Mezirow (1997) argues that significant 'life transitions' or crises create a disequilibrium that may then trigger 'transformational learning'. Fee and Gray use similar language to contextualise the learning that takes place on international placements describing it as following a, 'social, non-linear process, punctuated by a series of triggers that result in evolutionary

© The Author(s) 2017
H.L. Ackers et al., *Healthcare, Frugal Innovation, and Professional Voluntarism*, DOI 10.1007/978-3-319-48366-5_3

and revolutionary change' (Fee and Gray 2013). Other authors argue that the challenging and shocking nature of international placements in low-resource settings stimulates problem-solving, decision-making and coping skills (Kiernan et al. 2014; Longstaff 2012; Marçal-Grilo 2014). In the context of nursing education, Stephens describes the difficulty of trying to change student nurses' attitudes, values and behaviours. Using a meta-ethnography approach, she concludes that international placements constitute one of the most effective learning environments enabling nurses to move from 'compliance' through 'identification' to active 'internalisation' and behaviour change (2015: 1). Her analysis indicates that this is due to the combined dynamics of 'solving real problems', managing 'cultural encounters' and being forced out of one's 'comfort zone' (p. 7).

These sentiments are certainly echoed in the reports of respondents:

You go there and you're different and you hope that you're different when you come back. You can dress it up for other stuff but it's a whole different set of tasks and skills that I wanted to develop as a human being. [Nurse]

Staff come back motivated and inspired. They are more content in their own work, they feel very privileged and honoured to work in the NHS. [Line Manager]

I know why I became a doctor which I'd actually forgotten in the NHS. I'm going to go back to the NHS, I wasn't sure if I would go back to the NHS.

It takes some persistence and probing in interviews with returned volunteers to draw out specific competences and experiences. Before attempting to respond to this challenge, it is perhaps worth emphasising the fact that all learning is by nature difficult to capture, characterise and 'measure'.[1] This is particularly true of higher and more complex forms of knowledge or knowledge combinations blending explicit (perhaps clinical or engineering) skills with more tacit learning. Whilst we, as researchers, recognise the political and economic importance of specifying learning and its relevance and translational potential, we are also acutely aware that in trying to hold it fast and 'measure' it, we may understate its transformational qualities. Before examining the learning experiences of professional volunteers in more detail, we first consider the context within which this learning needs to evaluated, namely lifelong learning or continuing professional development systems within the NHS.

CONTINUING PROFESSIONAL DEVELOPMENT
IN THE NATIONAL HEALTH SERVICE

Training and professional development within the NHS, in common with most UK organisations, is managed and evaluated within the framework of *continuing professional development* (CPD). CPD is an important strategic tool for improving the effectiveness of the NHS workforce. The current annual allocation for Multi Professional Education and Training (MPET) in the NHS amounts to a staggering £4.9 billion (Health Education England 2016A). CPD in the NHS is not limited to the enhancement of individual clinical skill sets or career prospects; it is also a key mechanism to improve organisational effectiveness and patient outcomes. Sadler-Smith et al. (2000) identified three core functions of CPD. The *maintenance role*, which implies a generally passive and ongoing engagement with new workplace practices as they develop; the *survival role*, which enables practitioners to demonstrate their continued competence to work at an appropriate level; and the *mobility role*, which is essentially tied into an individual's aims and aspirations. This includes enhanced employability and career progression – potentially beyond their current employer. The Department of Health has long recognised the importance of CPD to NHS effectiveness, and all three strands of CPD are likely to be encountered within an arena as diverse as the NHS workforce. However, there is an acknowledgement that, in contrast to many other fields of employment, the rate of technological advancement and policy change in medicine and health care can be extremely rapid. This rapidity has a direct impact on working practices and means that there is an ever-present demand for healthcare professionals to review their knowledge and skills, and constantly engage with developments in their fields (i.e. an emphasis on *survival mode*).

As early as 2001, the framework for lifelong learning for the NHS was identifying how mandatory re-registration, post-registration and inter-professional education should focus on developing workforce skill sets (Department. of Health 2001). Until recently these types of initiative tended to have a clear clinical bias, focusing on developing and maintaining explicit, practical skills. In 2016, with the release of *Health Fit for the Future – Public Health People: A review of the public health workforce* (Public Health England 2016) the remit widened, and staff at all levels are now encouraged to engage with aspects of CPD that will 'enhance personal effectiveness skills, negotiating, influencing and co-production approaches' (Public Health England 2016), alongside specific technical skills. The Francis Report (2013) emphasised the importance of care and compassion at all levels of the NHS workforce. This stimulated a drive toward a 'value-based' strategy (Waugh et al. 2014) which has placed the '6 Cs'; Care, Compassion, Competence, Communication, Courage and Commitment (NHS 2016) at the heart of the NHS' skills enhancement agenda. As the NHS has attempted to utilise continuing professional development as a means of promoting productivity, innovation and efficiency so too has the emphasis shifted from more readily codified and measurable explicit skills to more complex and tacit transferable skills. The problems of codifying and measuring knowledge acquisition are as much a problem within the NHS environment as they are in sub-Saharan Africa.

## KNOWLEDGE MOBILISATION THROUGH PROFESSIONAL VOLUNTARISM

So, what kinds of knowledge and skills are enhanced through professional voluntarism? A recent report by the All-Party Parliamentary Group on Global Health, *Improving Health at Home and Abroad: How overseas volunteering from the NHS benefits the UK and the world* (APPG 2013), highlighted the scale and potential contribution of overseas volunteering to improving health globally and in the UK. The report is mainly concerned with the impact that NHS staff have on host settings but a degree of attention was also given to the advantages that staff themselves might derive, and the impact these will subsequently have on the organisation as a whole. The four primary areas of benefit outlined include the following:

1. Improving health in low-resource settings: volunteers are able to strengthen the capacity of health systems, institutions and professionals in these countries, where weaker training structures mean the chance to be supported by UK professionals is highly valued.
2. Leadership development: volunteers develop strong leadership skills and return with a greater understanding of how to enact change and communicate across professional cultures.
3. Sharing innovation: NHS staff are brought into direct contact with novel approaches to healthcare delivery, returning with greater confidence to challenge and change established practice in their Trust.

4. International relationships: a valuable asset to 'soft power' and international influence, giving Trusts a competitive advantage in recruitment and retention at home, and generating new opportunities for partnerships, research and revenue generation abroad. (APPG 2013)

Research on the experiences of healthcare professionals taking international placements suggests that a wealth of intense and valuable learning takes place. Many professionals describe developing a new perspective as a result of international placements (Jones et al. 2013; Wright et al. 2005). Others describe the development of specific skill sets such as communication, leadership and cultural awareness (Hockey et al. 2009; Lee et al. 2011; Norton and Marks-Maran 2014). A number of themes emerged from our literature review and empirical work with regard to 'what' learning happens and how this learning is facilitated. Before exploring these themes in more detail, it is important to emphasise that the majority of respondents cite a whole range of skills. The following response is typical:

I have come back with teaching skills, leadership skills, management, we have also done service development which the NHS want and I have been physically involved in the project and I think these are the skills that they want. I have achieved much more out here than I ever would at home. Not just a personal way, those hard skills are there. Clinically, if I was going to stay in paediatrics it has improved my neonatal examination skills. [In the UK] you can just order a test, they definitely improved and trying to think about language barriers and communication. And a realisation of how important building relationships is. [Junior Doctor]

This case illustrates the combination of explicit skills and the emphasis on core 'back-to-basics' clinical skills with transferable 'soft skills' in areas such as management and communication. This respondent also illustrates the quite common experience of using 'time out' on placement to help them make decisions about their future career development deciding to apply for general practitioner (community physician) positions on her return.

## CLINICAL SKILLS

Perhaps the most obvious (and potentially measurable) area of skills enhancement concerns explicit clinical skills (Kiernan et al. 2014). When asked about their motivations for applying for placements professional volunteers, especially doctors, refer immediately to the potential for clinical skills enhancement. And, post placement, professional volunteers report gains in clinical skills achieved through the sheer volume of cases they encounter; their exposure to diseases that are unusual in the UK; conditions that are rarely seen due to early or preventive intervention (the outcomes of delays) or, quite commonly, scenarios that they would have limited direct (hands-on) access to due to their status (in terms of seniority or cadre).

One of the most tangible and obvious benefits of spending time in a low-resource setting concerns the large volume of cases and the access that clinicians are likely to have, even at a relatively junior stage in their careers, to these. The idea that learning is gained through repetition (case volume) is captured by theories of learning focused on 'deliberative practice' which suggest that individuals acquire or hone skills through practice (Ericsson et al. 1993). Skills enhancement here relies on an assumption that the learner has been taught the skill in the first place, and it is use of that skill that perfects the skill and builds confidence in its utilisation; similarly, lack of practice may result in skills wastage or more likely in waning confidence. This form of learning, through repeated use of pre-existing skills, could arguably happen in the absence of supervision but may be significantly enhanced when the learner has access to a 'more knowledgeable person' (Kolb 1983; Nonaka and Takeuchi 1995).

An experienced midwife volunteer described the gains she feels she made in terms of clinical skills:

> Some of my clinical examination skills are ten times better than before we came out. In the UK we lose our basic skills and midwifery skills of how to palpate a uterus and to say which position the baby is lying in because if there's any doubt we just send for a scan. I had a woman who came and I felt her abdomen and she saw it on my face – she said, 'you think I've got two babies don't you?' I said, 'I really do think you've got two babies in there'. She laughed, she said she had a scan the week before and it said single baby but there were too many poles and too many limbs for it to be one baby. I said I'm not happy with that scan result I want you to go to [hospital] and have another scan and ring me. In the evening I got a telephone call. She said 'I have twins'! How fabulous that?

We have cited her at length here as the language she uses indicates not only the actual learning but also her sense of achievement and the confidence this has given her. A core clinical skill frequently mentioned by many volunteers from various cadres' concerns neonatal resuscitation:

I have resuscitated more babies in a few weeks here than in my whole career at home. There are times (in the UK) when the paediatrician is stuck in theatre or you're at a home birth and actually what do you do? Well you keep going (Midwife).

The midwife in this case points out the potential value of this on her return to the NHS either when staff are committed elsewhere or when she is at a home delivery. The effect of skills shortages combined with patient volume generates important opportunities to gain exposure in areas tangential to clinician's roles in the UK. We have noted a similar experience in relation to undergraduate electives (Ahmed, Ackers-Johnson and Ackers 2016) where students refer to opportunities for 'exposures' or 'spoking-out' from their main area of specialism. The following case involves a junior obstetrician:

I had not done any neonatal resuscitation until I came out here – obstetricians don't do neonatal resuscitation in the UK.

The opportunities for learning through repetition not only improve clinical skills but also enhance confidence in using those skills:

From a professional point of view, I've always had a gap...well not a gap...I'm not very confident and I should be more confident with neonatal resuscitation and care of the new-born.
Do you feel that you'll go back with confidence in neonatal resus?
Yeah, definitely, yeah.

This case illustrates the close relationships between actual skills and confidence in using those skills. In practice, it is hard to disentangle the two. The following anaesthetist makes a similar point about her exposure to working with children:

I have done a lot more paediatrics than I've ever done [in the UK] without supervision, so that is a clinical skill. I was anesthetising neonates.

The following doctor realised the benefits of this confidence when she returned to work in the NHS:

I have noticed that when I am on call at night – I know when I go to theatre there is pretty much nothing that can faze me; if I open for c/section I am pretty sure that whatever is there is not as bad as what I've done [in LMIC]. From a practical point of view that makes a big difference to your confidence.

One anaesthetic volunteer describes the patients he has encountered in a low-resource setting as 'sicker' than those he meets in the UK:

> The patients are generally sicker so it's a combination of factors. In certain clinical areas, you will de-skill, yes, but in other clinical areas it's a form of crash course, six months and then all your acute care skills as a physician you're just practicing them more commonly. You're less reliant on the high-tech stuff and you become more reliant on your clinical acumen.

These cases also illustrate the importance of volunteer learning in situations of emergency. The sheer volume of emergencies in these settings certainly provides critical learning across all specialities and a preparedness to think out of the box and react. One key informant referred specifically to this experience and the confidence it spawns:

> Their knowledge and skills are enhanced by what they've seen and they're more confident in responding to emergencies.

The volume of patients by definition implies a diversity of conditions and, sadly, in a low-resource setting characterised by extensive delays and poor patient management, exposure to conditions that are rarely witnessed in the UK. Kiernan et al. contend that the breadth and depth of conditions seen in low-resource settings provide exposure to a variety of illness allowing health workers to tap into a wider range of diagnoses. In the following case, a midwife refers to her experience with breech deliveries but also tropical diseases complicating normal pregnancies:

> From a purely medical point of view there is the opportunity to see a lot of conditions. I can do breech deliveries to get more skilled up in that – diseases in maternity so HIV, hepatitis in pregnancy, malaria, TB and that kind of stuff. . . . These things will be useful when I return in the UK.

A very experienced volunteer midwife who had spent time in a number of African countries returning to the UK in between argues that these skills could be very useful in the UK where the medicalisation of childbirth has (in her view) reduced patient choice:

> Can I just talk about clinical skills because I think that is really important – having been back and forth to Africa for a few years now, I have certainly

found that clinical skills say with breech and twins in the UK are really going downhill because everything goes to section. In the UK I see very often the obstetric distress where the person on call actually has not dealt with a breech or hasn't had much experience with twin deliveries. And they're the one who is getting really upset and stressed because the woman wants a vaginal delivery and that causes problems. To come here is actually an opportunity to witness and deliver twins where there is not that feeling that this woman must go for section or because you have a breech you must go to section. It is very much regarded as normal here.

Linking into the 'global health' discourse, the following volunteer notes that, although many of the conditions volunteers encounter are not common in the UK, they are increasingly relevant given high levels of immigration:

I have increased my knowledge of tropical diseases and malaria. I know it is not common in the UK but they do come up sometimes with people coming from other countries so it is nice to have that.

Obstetricians almost always report their experiences of serious complications that are either rarely seen in the UK (and they have only come across in textbooks) or that they would have limited direct access to in the UK due to their seniority:

I have had the opportunity to do complex cases here which are far different from the UK...there were plenty of uterine ruptures this week, multiple pregnancies and I had never done an ectopic pregnancy but I have now done that as well.

I will go home having done breach deliveries and lots of uterine rupture repairs. That will be two things on my obstetric CV that you won't have unless you do something like this.

One respondent expressed some concerns about the value of her new-found skills on return to the NHS where such complications were highly unusual:

I am not sure how these skills are transferable to my UK practice because I have been dealing with uterine rupture and some more obscure things and I'm not likely to see them for a long time in my practice in the UK if I ever do. I have been exposed to all sorts of clinical scenarios.

A leading representative of the Royal College of Obstetricians responded to these concerns in an SVP workshop re-assuring volunteers that these skills are relevant and, furthermore, often lacking among NHS consultants:

> The skills you are learning are fantastic and actually the majority of UK consultants could not do any of these things you have just mentioned because they have never seen them and that is a huge risk to the mothers in the UK. We are seeing maternal deaths occurring because the people just don't have that experience which the previous consultants may never have seen before. That demonstrates something in you – that your experience allows you to confidently say, 'well somebody has to do it' while in the UK people don't seem to have that and they are frightened of doing that. So if you are given that confidence to actually deal with the situation which you are presented with this is hugely valuable. You may not use it in ten years but that 1 in 10 years – that is very important.

The opportunities for clinical learning will vary by cadre and placements may not provide opportunities for all people or in all skills. And, from that point of view, it may be difficult for them to map neatly and comprehensively onto a comprehensive CPD framework. Anaesthetists, for example, often report fewer opportunities for the kinds of clinical skills enhancement that is immediately relevant to their practice in the UK. This reflects the fact that the equipment and gases used are so different:

> Clinically it won't be cutting edge things that I've learned but I've learned how to use drugs that I haven't used before, like ketamine which I've never used in the UK.

Other anaesthetic volunteers immediately identify skills applications in the UK:

> The clinical skills I've learnt? I don't normally use ketamine back in the UK; I've never used the anaesthetic agent ether or halothane before and so you're using all these drugs but some of them are available in the UK. Some are not but the ones that are you'll be so much more skilled in using them. I'll even go as far as saying I know people that are so much more senior than me at consultant level that have never used drugs that I've used that I could make useful in settings back in the UK. They've gone on to become established consultants and they may have only seen one or zero cases. Some of the cases you see out here as a registrar level anaesthetist sure

you won't see those commonly again in the UK, and if you do, something has seriously gone wrong but the skills you learn are very transferable, very transferable to other conditions and you're incredibly more confident.

In the following example, a junior doctor distinguishes learning in surgical skills from internal medicine:

> I think the people who learn the most from this experience will be internal medicine which is not surgery, just because of the array of things they see over there, people usually present very advanced malaria and how to treat it, I mean I don't know how you would apply that [in the UK] but it increases infectious disease knowledge. They would see more advanced TB that could be applied over here now. They can see very advanced things. From the anaesthetic and surgery point of view, we see things like very advanced cancer, someone with a huge tumour, something that could have been solved earlier. Things are more scary and exciting, you don't have as much modern equipment, you have to make do and adapt to your patient. You learn so much.

In such cases, skills enhancement may be constrained by the lack of access to essential equipment, consumables or cultures of practice. Indeed, in many situations, clinical intervention may simply be impossible due to these environmental factors. The prevalence of these kinds of situation led to the development of the THET-funded bio medical engineering project designed specifically to reduce the occasions on which interventions are limited by lack of usable equipment.[2] As well as improving local health systems this project has enhanced opportunities for volunteer learning by keeping theatres, neonatal units and high dependency units operational. Equipment is not always the main factor. One mid-career obstetrician suggested that, from a narrow clinical perspective, his skills were not being enhanced because 'here there is nothing between a normal delivery and a c-section – they don't do assisted deliveries and that is where a lot of the skill lies'.

This in part (and at face value) reflected a lack of equipment but in fact reflects a much deeper seated cultural[3] opposition to the use of forceps or vacuum for assisted delivery. In another case an ophthalmologist suggested that in his specialism, experiencing new diseases was a less significant component of overall learning:

> In ophthalmology, I don't think the primary benefit for medical staff is that you will see unusual things because most blindness in [LMICs] is cataracts and squints and we've plenty of those ourselves. So I don't think seeing new

diseases – that's not a big issue. You might see a more advanced case of something you already know but that in itself is neither here nor there.

Certainly, as managers of professional volunteers, we were aware that placing some cadres presented greater immediate challenges that would affect clinical learning. Where a specialism is underdeveloped or even non-existent, it is more difficult to relate clinical skills learning directly to CPD frameworks at home. Mental health is a case in point. One mental health nurse suggested that her learning was less focused on improving clinical skills and much more focused on 'soft' skills.[4]

We have referred (above) to 'exposures' outside health workers' disciplinary specialisms. In many cases these exposures have played quite an influential role in helping volunteers to make decisions about their future careers – or adding to their CVs to make those decisions possible. The following junior doctor used the opportunity to gain experience in midwifery as the basis for a planned specialism in obstetrics:

> I'm almost certainly going to go into obstetrics training when I get back so for now I'm still quite a general doctor. It's good experience for me, practically it's a lot of hands on stuff, I'm doing a lot of midwifery work – it's useful to have that basic background isn't it? When I say basic that's a bit rude really, I just mean it will be useful to know how things should work normally compared to when things go wrong so that's really useful. Already I'm much better at delivering babies than I was two months ago so that's brilliant, that's really fun and satisfying.

The SVP social science volunteer, involved in evaluation, later decided to train as a nurse in the UK. In another case, a more experienced midwife used the opportunity to gain access to management experience which she felt would help her to make the next step in her career:

> It depends what stage in your career you are as well, I don't need to go and learn clinically really. I'm looking to stop working totally clinically (to work) in management.

Sadly, the exposure to acute situations also results in very immediate experiences of mortality:

> I have looked after ladies with more still births in the six months I have been here than I have ever in my whole career. In the UK, people are absolutely

mortified even if they have a late miscarriage. It's so upsetting. If they have a stillborn it's devastating. You know huge counselling and just horrendous.

The immediate and repeated experience of mortality constitutes a key component of risk in volunteer management and must be managed accordingly. However, it does also present opportunities for skills development in terms of counselling skills and resilience; these are often also linked to elements of cultural awareness (see below).

Whilst the opportunities generated through patient volume or disease complexity will doubtless generate novel exposures for UK health professionals, the quality of the training environment may reduce the potential for knowledge gains. A key factor here is supervision. Where junior or non-specialist staff are exposed to situations without access to adequate mentoring or supervision skills enhancement will not be optimised. Indeed, the level of absenteeism of staff and especially doctors in low-resource settings (Ackers et al. 2016) can significantly reduce the clinical exposure of professional volunteers as theatres remain closed for extensive periods. The following junior doctor refers to the need for clinical supervision in low-resource settings and the importance of having a UK mentor to compensate for the lack of immediate supervision:

It becomes a challenge when you have a baby that you don't know what to do and you don't, at the health centre, have someone to discuss that baby with and I've emailed my mentor about a couple of babies and have had to rely on a senior doctor from the UK rather than having a senior doctor here. So in terms of co-presence I mentioned that I am not always working with a doctor but I am always working in co-presence with the nurse in charge of that unit. I do think for junior doctors, you do need a doctor that you can talk to about cases.

Literature on learning theories describes the importance of a 'more knowledgeable other' to some forms of learning (Vygotsky 1988) which enables the learner to move from the 'zone of current development' to the 'zone of proximal development' (Harland 2003). According to this theory, the 'more knowledgeable other' could be someone from other professional cadre; what is significant is that they have a higher skill set on that specific aspect of knowledge.

This is a point we pick up in Chapter 4 and reflect the potential tensions between optimising the skills of volunteers and minimising the damage to health systems caused by unintended consequences (Ackers and Ackers-Johnson 2016). In the absence of effective safeguards, professional volunteers may also be exposed to unacceptable levels of risk through lone working in such circumstance, a point we return to later.

## LEADERSHIP

Leadership is notoriously difficult to pin down both as a discrete skill and as an element in self-reported assessment. The lack of clarity around the concept was pointed out over 40 years ago (Sales 1966), and many attempts have been made to disaggregate its components (see, for example, Tourangeau and McGilton 2004; Rohs and Langone 1997). In terms of professional placements and international volunteering, the hypothetical construct of leadership is often referred to as if it were a homogeneous concept. Even the Chartered Institute of Personnel Development brackets elements as diverse as time management and creativity under the rubric of 'leadership skills' (CIPD 2014). At policy level, there is also ambiguity. The 2010 framework for NHS involvement in international development (NHS and DoH 2010), for example, singles out the development of 'leadership' as a key strategic priority. The 2013 All-Parliamentary Group on Global Health similarly refers to volunteers developing 'strong leadership skills', and returning from their overseas encounters with 'a greater understanding of how to enact change and communicate across professional cultures' (APGGH 2013). So, in this case, there is a conflation of leadership skills with cultural competency.

Many NHS policy documents outline the requirement of NHS staff to demonstrate leadership skills. The NHS '5 Year Forward View' document has a focus on leadership (NHS England 2014). Additionally, the '2022 GP' has a focus on co-ordinating complex care and the role that general practitioners play in coordinating multidisciplinary skills. The Health and Care Professionals Council (HCPC) standards of proficiency suggests physiotherapists, psychologists and radiologists should understand the concept of leadership and be able to apply it to practice. Furthermore, leadership is named as one of eight principles of nursing practice by the Royal College of Nursing (2015).

Clearly leadership is recognised as a core skill across the NHS and an ability to demonstrate leadership is necessary and desirable in staff of all professions and all career stages. If it were well-evidenced that international placements develop these skills, then it could provide a way to increase human resource capital, at a time when maximising staff skills is increasingly important.

Furthermore, the NHS Leadership academy has created numerous frameworks to help assess leadership in healthcare professionals. The medical leadership competency framework (MLCF) was devised in 2008 and aims to identify competencies that need to be developed and can be used by any NHS professional (Hockey et al. 2009). The model includes five domains: personal qualities, setting direction, working with others, improving services and managing services. It has been argued that this framework, along with others, can be applied to work in low-resource settings to develop leadership. In a specific project involving UK professionals working in Cambodia with a purpose of leadership development, authors argue that having complete ownership of a healthcare improvement project enables professionals to engage in processes of planning, management, critical evaluation, systematic enquiry and encouraging innovation (Hockey et al. 2009).

Available literature suggests that professional volunteers based in low-resource settings are presented with opportunities to lead that they would otherwise not have in the NHS (Baguley et al. 2006; Banatvala and Macklow-Smith 1997; Jones et al. 2013; Kiernan et al. 2014). Many of our respondents describe being in a low-resource environment as a catalyst for them to acquire leadership skills, out of necessity. As noted above, the kinds of skills or experiences they identify are quite diverse ranging from elements of project management, health systems thinking, quality improvement, audit and cross-cultural, inter-professional communication within teams frequently involving conflict management. Some volunteers, often at a more advanced stage in their careers, identify this as a specific objective of their placement to gain management experience to support career development on their return. Others become involved in high-level project management initiatives. The first case presented below involves a registrar who was in part motivated to volunteer in order to gain management skills. She identifies the difficulty she has had in the UK in gaining this kind of experience, even though, according to her, this forms an explicit component of her training:

> It is difficult as a registrar in the UK to really get involved in management...there is management stuff in my training; there are specific things that I have to do. You don't really get a lot of say in how things

are running and should happen.... and I mean that is the way forward
to try and get the team we were working with to think about new ideas.
I think that would be good to try and do that before I become a
consultant rather than after.

In this case, the doctor developed a large triage area in the national referral
hospital. Whilst this may sound relatively straightforward from a UK
perspective, triage is one of the most difficult concepts to introduce in
LMIC settings (see Ackers et al. 2016, for a case study of this process).
The next respondent refers specifically to the emphasis on managing
'dysfunctional teams' in her training and the experience she has gained:

> Lots of management, I'm sure it will make me better at managing a team
> where all is not going as it should do. That's one thing that's on my
> advanced training modules 'how to manage a dysfunctional team'.

As noted above, many quite junior volunteers engaged directly in managing complex interventions. Arguably this type of experience is likely to be
more prevalent in volunteering positions that are focused on capacity-
building rather than service delivery per se as these often encourage
volunteers to develop or work within multi-professional teams. In such
cases and especially where projects are funded, placements will have an
emphasis on evaluation and audit. The SVP evaluation identified many
situations in which early career health workers became actively involved in
management and leadership for the first time in their careers. The respondent in the next case immediately linked her own experience of project
management as an early career obstetrician to evidence of personal qualities
such as initiative and responsibility:

> It shows initiative. How you can cope in such situations. I got a level of
> responsibility that I would never have got in the UK working in project
> management and leadership. It shows that I have more skills.

In the two following cases, quite junior doctors (pre-specialisation)
achieved a high level of engagement with staff and very senior managers
setting them apart from their peers at home:

> From the professional point of view it's benefitted me. Obviously something
> I've never done before and it's really more on the coordination and

management of people. I feel like I am actually benefitting a great deal from coordinating different people. We are meeting people even up to directorship level who are inputting lots of quite useful ideas and I'm meeting guys who are meeting at a technical level within a low-resource setting which is something that I was never used to, so this is also quite beneficial to me professionally. I think I'll be stronger from here, professionally.

I am much more experienced than my grading as a doctor. I spent time on wards to train a great many staff and I am much more comfortable in different settings and difficult situations. Now, I have seen it before and have done it before in different circumstances. I got different skills in leadership and in people management. [But] communication was the main place where I learned lots of extra skills.

Volunteers were acutely aware that these are the kinds of skills that are highly prized in the NHS or at least in NHS rhetoric and believed that their ability to concretely evidence them is likely to accelerate their career progression. In the following case the doctor refers to the systems thinking components of this experience and the link to organisational innovation:

Things like managing people, leadership, quality improvement projects especially as you get more senior. That's what consultants want to see when you are applying for a job, they don't need to know that you can hold an airway because that's competency, they want to see that you can see a health system and innovate, how you can improve something, and I think that's something that I would say to my Deanery when they ask what I learned from this.

She also uses the language of 'quality Improvement' as a component of management. Quality improvement emerged in other volunteer accounts. In the next case the respondent links this closely to inter-personal and inter-cultural skills. She also makes direct reference to the value of learning from failure:

I've done a few quality improvement projects which have been a real obstacle and I've come to learn how you have to strategize, deal with different personalities, when to move forward, when to stop and observe so a lot of inter personal and inter cultural skills that I've had to learn. I've also learned about myself, to understand myself more, ask myself why I am frustrated.

Some volunteers talk of leadership in a more routine way in terms of managing difficult trainees and the use of diplomacy to instil behaviour change:

> Its leadership, service development and communication where I've learned a lot. I think my people handling skills; I've got an intern who is particularly difficult to manage. I'm trying to get the best out of him, those kinds of skills have come on a lot.

> Interpersonal skills that you're drawing on every minute of the day; trying to get things done in a diplomatic fashion.

The following respondent suggests that her experience of managing change will be of direct value to the NHS and impress her managers far more than gains in clinical skills that may arise from placements in high-resource settings:

> What they will be very interested in, what they will see in me is an individual who is very motivated to try to change things in spite of a very difficult environment, and if she is able to do that, if she comes to our Trust and we give her a project/protocol to start to improve things, she would be the one. I think they will appreciate that more than say if I went to America and learned a new fancy skill.

This area of learning, especially for those cadres with little previous exposure to leadership, could be interpreted as an example of 'experiential learning' which Ng et al. (2009) characterise as a 'holistic process of adapting to the world'. Patrick describes experiential learning as, 'learning through reflection on doing' (Patrick 2011). Arguably, this kind of learning can continue to happen effectively in the absence of co-present supervision (Kolb 1983), although this learning process will vary according to the environment and qualities of the learner.

Whilst many respondents talk about leadership and management in terms of people management skills, others referred to the experience they had gained in resource management more generally. Low-resource settings are characterised by major problems in terms of consumables and medicine management. This by no means only concerns the lack of resources per se but very poor systems resulting in regular stock-outs further compounded by endemic and highly innovative corruption. It is by no means unusual to see theatre lists closed due to a lack of surgical gloves, theatre linen or basic equipment or triage halted due to the lack of blood pressure machines. Inevitably professional volunteers become involved in these processes on a daily basis:

> I've gained skills and expertise related to logistics, resources and stores, stocks and supplies and all those kind of things that really could be useful.

As Crisp (2010) notes, managing resources is as much a problem for high income settings and the NHS as it is for low-income settings such as Bangladesh, and there are great opportunities for knowledge transfer and frugal innovation. The NHS' '5 year Forward View' suggests innovative ideas for cost saving are important and that these should be implemented more quickly in the future (National Health Service England 2014). Evidence suggests that placements in low-resource settings improve awareness of the relative costs of interventions and the damaging effects of resource misuse (Kiernan et al. 2014; Leather et al. 2010). The phrase 'problem-solving' is used throughout the reviewed literature to describe a skill set that develops as a result of international placements (Baguley et al. 2006; Horton 2009; Longstaff 2012). The interviews link this financial awareness to 'back to basics' clinical skills and problem solving:

> I Had to Use My Eyes, My Ears and My Stethoscope like I've Never Done Before.

> We're so used to ordering investigations, we've forgotten some of those basic skills.

The development of soft skills can be seen as a key facilitator in the various stages of clinical skill development. For example, planning, concentration, repetition and revision (a tendency to practice), study style and reflection (a tendency to self-regulate learning). The next two cases show how a resource constrained environment improves the ability to plan and solve problems:

> I've become more resourceful because of the lack of resources and equipment that works. I've learned to anticipate what's ahead and what might go wrong and get myself ready for it, whereas back home I have an assistant so I don't have to worry. So it makes me prepare and not rely on anyone else. [Anaesthetic volunteer]

I learned to be more resourceful, clinically, because if something bad happens, there's no one else. It taught me to how to monitor patients even with the most minimal equipment especially with kids and I think that's quite a useful skill. [F2 doctor]

The next case is very typical and refers to the awareness that volunteers gain from their core skills. We have used the word awareness here as in many cases this is not about developing new skills but remembering and revitalising skills. In this example the bio medical engineer volunteer is talking about the fundamental science that lies at the heart of his profession but lies dormant in the UK:

It's made me think about things completely differently. About the way I work in the NHS particularly in times of resource constraints and trying to think laterally about the way you do things. It makes you go back and think about things in their fundamentals... of course physics and that kind of thing. UK degrees are fantastic but they are so theoretical.

The MOVE project did not set out to capture the views of line managers as such. However, some returned volunteers had themselves become line managers as in the following case:

Low-resource settings give people the ability to think on their feet and be quicker and I think they become people who can solve things; people who are used to working in high resource setting, I don't think they are very flexible – especially when you have worked somewhere like Australia or New Zealand where health care is very prescriptive and very defined (Midwifery Lead)

One of the line managers interviewed was involved with the recruitment of Army reservists and their deployment to low-resource settings usually in crisis situations. He was very clear about the skills they were offering potential recruits and the NHS:

The organisational skills are gonna be first and foremost. These people will have to stretch themselves clinically with the things they are dealing with and bring this clinical practice back to the UK. So we've seen catastrophic traumatic situations that are influencing how we deliver care back in the NHS. We'll offer you leadership, we'll give you confidence in presenting and all that sort of stuff cos you've got to be quite credible, so all of these things will give you an edge. When we're dealing with the NHS we find that senior managers straight away see the benefits of reserve service. You send us someone with clinical ability and we'll enhance that ability in a wider field than you do. We'll give you back somebody who's very comfortable with sorting order from chaos, being in a stressful situation and able to manage people and lead teams. That's quite an ambitious statement to make, but that's what we deliver.

This statement echoes the literature on highly skilled mobility generally and scientific mobility, in particular. In this context mobility is often seen as a way of recruiting the 'brightest and the best' or those individuals more willing to take risk and innovate. Nevertheless, we must allow for the fact that those individuals who put themselves forward for professional placements in low-resource settings (all else being equal) may be a self-selecting group. And, added to that, recruitment and deployment processes may identify individuals with a high degree of resilience and ethical commitment. The following volunteer hints at such:

I don't know if you have to be a tough person already to some degree?

Another volunteer talks of how she is no longer afraid of 'risky situations' – the question is whether organisations recruit people who are less risk averse or whether the process itself develops this quality. Certainly, the recruitment processes that volunteer deployment organisations are involved in will actively valorise resilience.

Leadership and management are necessarily linked to team working. The NHS and its training arm (Health Education England) have recently placed significant emphasis on the development of multidisciplinary teams and the dissolution of counter-productive professional boundaries (HEE 2016C). Kiernan et al. (2014) suggest that international placements provide unique opportunities to work with people from other professions. This finding is echoed by professional volunteers who describe the skills they gain through team working with other cadres. This arises in a number of ways. First, deploying organisations may actively mobilise multi-professional teams in complex interventions. This is the case both in systems-focused capacity-building environments and humanitarian crisis situations. Secondly, volunteers witness the stark absence of team-working in hosting organisations which heightens their awareness of its value. And, thirdly, the act of simply living in proximity to other volunteers from diverse backgrounds undermines professional boundaries as the following case illustrates:

> It's great that teams go out there that are multi-disciplinary because you see your colleagues in a different way and appreciate their roles more. You are all in it together when you're out in a difficult situation. I mean it's so resource poor that it is actually a hard thing to go and live in an environment where it's not a guarantee that water will come out of a tap or you plug something in and it will work. That's quite difficult really, so I think you see people rather than colleagues.

We have made the point on several occasions that active learning in low-resource settings often comes about as a direct result of observing or experiencing failure. This is also the case with regard to team-working where the challenge of solving immediate problems precipitates a team dynamic:

> When they go and realise the absence of team work [there] it makes them aware that they do do team working (in the UK) and they realise how important team working is. [Line Manager]

Team working was also specifically emphasised in the interviews with army reservists:

> Certainly one thing about the military is team work, because everybody just works as a team and just does it. There is no premadonnas. And that team work, if you could bring that team work back that is what you would want to bring back. [to the NHS]

Volunteers often report positive experiences while working in local teams. Key among these was a heightened appreciation of the damaging effects of professional hierarchies and boundaries. This was not because such boundaries are any less evident in low-resource settings which are often more hierarchical (Briscoe 2013). It was more closely related to dimensions of positionality[5] and the uniquely privileged status that volunteers acquire – as supernumerary foreigners – which positions even quite junior health workers in critical leadership roles.

Many volunteers become involved in aspects of audit, protocol development and related training (Ackers et al. 2016). This broad area of skills could be categorised as a component of teaching or research (see below) but also forms a key component of leadership in the NHS. The 'Trainee Doctor' underlines the importance of accurate and clear clinical records and understanding the principles and practice of infection control (General Medical Council 2009). Working in low-resource settings exposes professionals to the stark reality and consequences of lack of compliance with clinical guidelines and protocols, especially in areas such as patient management and infection prevention control. Standage and Randall (2014) argue that working overseas provides nurses with a greater understanding of why it is necessary to do things that are required in the NHS such as gaining a child's consent by experiencing an environment in which such systems are not in place. Nurses on international placements become critical observers of the difference in the implementation of safety procedures such as infection control (Button et al. 2005). Some returned individuals reported that experiencing a world without NHS standards, allowed them to appreciate their importance (Greatrex-White 2008). Certainly the ethnographic work with SVP volunteers shows that almost every volunteer when confronted with the chaos that is present in most public health facilities immediately jumps to advocate interventions focused on patient management, record-keeping, audit, infection prevention control and surgical safety (Ackers et al. 2016). The stimulus for this comes from the immediate and stark reality of outcomes associated with its absence. Patient safety is an ongoing theme in most interventions and the spectre of Ebola/Marburg pushes this home:

It just made me think in terms of patient safety in this environment.

## LEARNING FROM FAILURE

At a pragmatic level, it is argued that learning experiences embedded in the context of a developing country provide invaluable opportunities for staff to see the consequences of poor healthcare system management. The senior manager of a charity providing volunteer placements in Africa told us:

I was talking recently to some returned mental health nurses who were learning about the side effects of the drugs that are given to schizophrenics. But when they went to Africa they actually saw the side effects of these drugs that they never see here – patients foaming at the mouth and whatever. And they saw the end stage of things that would've been dealt with much earlier her. And that's very dramatic, but on a different level, I think that a lot of people in the NHS get sick to the back teeth of paper pushing. Then as soon as they get to a developing country, and see really chaotic health care and the first thing they want to do is paper push because they understand the real value of audit and basic patient management, of basic triage. They get to see how badly things go wrong if those systems aren't in place, that I guess on a routine day to day over here might seem a bit boring – maybe even unnecessary. But they see the lack of audit and the consequences of basic patient observations and patient notes. They see the value of interventions that they take for granted here, and they see the consequences of stuff that doesn't work.

The absence of the highly ordered societal and organisational structures that we are so used to in the West was mentioned by many people who had worked in low-resource settings. A fundamental lack of basic administration systems in many settings could be difficult to come to terms with. This appeared to be especially frustrating for nursing staff who tend to be known for their reliance on securely structured protocols, and were used to working in the 'protocol heavy' environment of the HNS. A placement provider told us how she had noticed that while there was a general culture of negativity towards the opaque layers of bureaucracy which tend to characterise the NHS, when staff returned from locations that did not have even the basics of such systems they often found a renewed appreciation for them and: '... the first thing they want to do is an audit.'

Barbara was a senior clinical manager and part of a team who regularly travelled to Central Africa to provide training courses in emergency obstetric care. She told us how the complete lack of structure in many of the health centres she had encountered still shocked her, even after many trips. This lack of structure could extend well beyond the clinical environments that she and her team needed to engage with:

They don't register births, deaths, marriages. It just happens. Which is such an alien thing to us in a country where I think we have an image of who's here – we know how many are here – you know with all the information that we gather when we do a census we've got a good grasp on what we think our population is, whereas in Africa that doesn't exist. Patient records are hit and miss. They may have a record, they may not. So it's very difficult because when somebody dies there's a process that we have to go through of reporting it and making sure the right forms are filled in. It just doesn't happen there. It's just give them back to the relative and off they go. Without it [medical bureaucracy], although it feels like a lot of red tape and it feels like a barrier to giving the care that we want to give, but it actually gives us so much more than that, just on that level of a process, although it is sort of a name and a number, it gives that person some value. And I think it's different when you go to Africa, it makes you feel a bit vulnerable because you could just disappear. Nobody would look, and nobody would even know that you existed.

The absence of good teamwork in some settings was also reported, but even this could be seen as an important learning opportunity:

> It's learning through the observation of failure. I don't think they're going there and seeing wonderfully good practice or team working or patient safety. When people learn over here [in the UK] and when people prepare learning materials, they show them best practice, and all the examples are best practice. That's not what they see in developing countries. They see dreadful practice, but it shocks them into very simple back to basics thinking. Things like 'no one took that patient's temperature' or 'no one made a note of that'. And I think 98 per cent of what they're doing is learning from and reacting to bad practice. [Placement charity worker]

Many volunteers comment on the level of bureaucracy in the NHS and its impact on clinical time; but at the same time most engage in some form of protocol development and audit. In the following case the respondent is planning to use her new skills as soon as she returns home to a new role:

> I've just got a new job doing audit which will be really interesting. I'm hopefully going to use some of that here as well.

Witnessing the outcomes of bad practice and lack of clinical guidelines also makes volunteers aware of the role that these processes play in promoting justice for patients:

> I try to look at things from another positive perspective, it makes me much more tolerant of a lot of bureaucracy because I think well at least we do have that level of protection somebody will pay attention if reported something in

the UK and that I think is right – somebody will listen and there is some system that to try and get some justice in some way

Having said that there is often a sense among volunteers that returning to the NHS will undermine their new found autonomy and weigh them down with what they view as excessive administration:

How are you feeling about returning to the NHS?
To be honest it fills me with a bit of dread, as much as things are tough here and frustrating, sometimes when you save lives here it really hits home and its more rewarding but I do miss the efficiency, but I don't want to go back to administrative paper work and that's what the NHS is heading towards. And over here I have more freedom with my ideas and back home it's a lot more structured and there's so many levels of authority and administration for someone to ok you.

The empirical data generated as part of the MOVE project supports existing literature to suggest significant and accelerated (intense) exposure to managerial and leadership skills on placement in low-resource settings. Unfortunately, the paucity of research that exists suggests that these competencies may fail to support effective knowledge mobilisation in the NHS on their return due to a lack of leadership options or systems closure. The engagement of often very early career professionals (and even students) in leadership roles often reflects the fact that volunteers find themselves to be the most senior person in the facility, or are perceived by local staff to be in such a position. This carries both opportunities and risks and raises questions about supervision and responsibility (Dowell and Merrylees 2009).

## COMMUNICATION

The ability to communicate is a key skill in any and every workplace especially when dealing with customers and patients. Guidance from the Nursing and Midwifery Council (2012) identifies 'poor communication skills' as a common area of concern with regard to fitness to practice and the General Medical Council (2009) emphasises the need for 'Tomorrows Doctors' to communicate appropriately in different circumstances. These concerns are echoed in the Health Professions Council assertion that physiotherapists and psychologists should be able to communicate effectively using both verbal and non-verbal methods and understanding the impact of culture on these. Communication is also one of the '6C's' (NHS England 2014). This document focuses on the centrality of communication in care, specifically that decisions should not be made about the patient without their consent; it also has a focus on the importance of listening.

Much of the literature describes how communication skills are enhanced during international placements (Kiernan et al. 2014). This argument centres around the development of skills to communicate with people from a different culture/country, such as overcoming language barriers, developing non-verbal communication and communicating in a culturally sensitive manner. Furthermore, the development of a generic 'communication' skills set is stated throughout many of the articles found in the systematic review (Jones et al. 2013; Kiernan et al. 2014; Lee et al. 2011; Norton and Marks-Maran 2014). Whilst most literature talks in general terms, some break this down into more specific learning. Norton and Marks-Maran (2014), for example, refer to the development of 'interpersonal skills to live and work together with people of all nationalities and cultures' and Duffy et al. suggest that simply being in a foreign culture is the most important facilitator of learning in an international environment. Clampin (2008) argues that being in another environment and outside your comfort zone forces individuals to reconsider their existing methods of communication and this results in novel approaches.

The majority of professional volunteers interviewed identified 'communication' amongst the key areas of learning. This embraced a range of skills including verbal and non-verbal skills and involving patients and/or colleagues. Many of the respondents had worked in countries where English is the language used at work (amongst professionals). In these cases, their learning often reflected a heightened awareness of how, even when using English, communication presents a challenge. This may reflect the type of English used or its combination with other forms of non-verbal communication. Volunteers become acutely aware of how problematic communication can be even when they share a common language:

> You are developing different communication skills – different people, different cultural norms. They speak very good English but you have got to communicate in a different way to make yourself clearly understood so communication is a big thing. The knowledge and skills framework is about communication, equality and diversity – all those kind of things.

Although much of the literature emphasises communication from a health worker-patient interface, volunteers speak more about communication with other health workers in multidisciplinary and often international environments. The following volunteer uses the language of diplomacy to characterise these skills:

> The non-technical skills are the most prominent thing; the interpersonal skills that you're drawing on every minute of the day trying to get things done in a diplomatic fashion.

In other cases respondents spoke of the challenges of communicating with patients through the use of translators; an experience that will be of great value on their return to the UK. In other contexts communication skills were closely aligned with leadership and negotiation skills and networking with key stakeholders outside of their disciplinary specialisms:

> I've learnt about the networking thing really; approaching people in different ways, like someone who is political, you also meet him as a politician. To break that ice.

The cases above suggest an emphasis not so much on communication with patients but more on the role that professional volunteers play as knowledge intermediaries or brokers (Ackers et al. 2016) spanning the boundaries between different cadres of staff or levels of seniority or the interface between health workers and health planners and stakeholders. Peate (2008) similarly identifies the importance of communication skills for negotiation whilst Banatvala and Macklow-Smith (1997) refer to communication as affecting the ability to liaise between diverse groups. The following example illustrates these boundary spanning skills and their value to a hierarchical NHS:

> I often didn't ask the name of the scrub nurse because I never thought it would be relevant to me, I never thought I'd want to know the name of the guy who's pushing the trolley in and out of corridors. But you come here and realise actually just by getting to know the cleaner which you may not do back in the UK so just building those personal, professional relationships with people can make a big difference to your outcome. I'm starting a job in a new hospital now [in the NHS] and I'm going to make a lot more effort to get to know the people I'm working with.

The relative lack of reference to their communication skills with patients may reflect the overwhelming emphasis on inter-professional relationships in many international placements rather than the fact that volunteers do not experience or learn about communicating with patients. Our ethnographic experience of working with professional volunteers suggests that the stark absence of attention to communication with patients in low-resource settings is in itself a huge learning process. In the Ugandan public health context (which needs to be differentiated from the private sector), for example, it is very usual to see no verbal communication taking place between health workers and patients or to witness verbal abuse. In that respect, volunteers are learning through the observation of bad practice and often find this aspect of learning quite stressful.

## Cultural Awareness

In an increasingly diverse British society, much of the literature stresses the increasing importance of adapting to the needs of individuals from other cultures. Between 1993 and 2014 the number of foreign-born individuals living in the UK almost doubled from 7% to 13%, suggesting there is an increasing need for NHS staff to be able to best serve the needs of migrant populations. The General Medical Council's 'Tomorrows Doctors' suggests that doctors should understand the sociological factors that contribute to illness, course of disease and treatment success, including the effect of poverty (GMC 2009). The Royal College of Surgeons' 'Good Surgical Practice' suggests that encounters with patients and colleagues should be culturally sensitive and non-discriminatory. Similar commitments are expressed by the Nursing and Midwifery Council (NMC 2015). International placements provide an excellent opportunity for staff to experience other cultures and develop cultural awareness (Leather et al. 2010).

Respondents also emphasised this area of learning and its relationship with personal qualities such as patience and tolerance:

> The value of working with the team, managing other people, looking at your own expectations and how you view patients and other members of staff. Taking into account other cultures, other perspectives. It broadens you as a person and it makes you more tolerant.

The reference here to patience and tolerance is very common. In the next case the volunteer nurse suggests that being out of her 'immediate comfort zone' will improve her empathy on return:

> You come back and you are a bit more generous with your time, a bit more understanding, a bit more empathetic with people from different backgrounds. We see everybody in all walks of life in the NHS and sometimes despite all our training in equality and diversity let's face it y'know we can have some inbuilt kind of prejudice against whatever it is and I think that it helps break those down. It makes you broader minded.

It is clear from the above that cultural knowledge, skills and attitudes are extremely important to team working and service delivery in the National Health Service. It is interesting to reflect at this juncture on the issue of cosmopolitanism and heterogeneity. The UK is in many respects far more cosmopolitan and diverse than many of the locations professional volunteers will find themselves in especially if they have experience of working in the larger multi-ethnic urban areas. Our experience as researchers on the ground would suggest that it is not so much the exposure to new cultures that precipitates the acute learning that takes place but the profound sense and experience of being an outsider themselves and reflecting on their own identity and people's perceptions of them:

> The soft skills you learn are huge and valuable because you are doing it in a different culture as the outsider, and constantly working at five different ways of asking something silly. I think those kinds of skills you don't find [in your own culture] I can't imagine getting them at that level in such a short period of time.

Norton and Marks-Maran (2014) describe 'cultural awareness' as the exploration of one's own cultural and professional background, including recognising one's biases, prejudices and assumptions about individuals who are different. Briscoe (2013) similarly argues that cultural sensitivity develops out of self-awareness and an ability to critically reflect; immersion in an international context may encourage a growth in self-awareness and critical thinking that underpins genuine cultural awareness. This point is illustrated in the next two cases both of which refer to communication with peers rather than patients as such. In the first case the respondent explains how her training and experience in the UK failed to prepare her for her own experience of being an 'outsider':

> The first half of the placement was an eye opener. Certainly in the UK you're kind of aware of all the cultural differences and you 'do' equal opportunities but until you're actually in a place where you're the outsider, you don't realise how much it impacts, so I've gained non clinical skills such as communication and cultural awareness.

In the next example the volunteer is herself a third country national employed in the NHS. She suggests that whilst her own experience as an outsider in the NHS has increased her awareness of cultural difference, she has gained in communication skills:

> I am from Thailand so for me I am used to it and can integrate but I think it's a very useful skill for people. It's really important, in any job communication is so important and in the UK there are so many different cultures, it does help for communication.

In the next example the respondent talks about her experiences as a 'mzungu' (white person) in sub-Saharan Africa:

> Personal skills, how to deal with the frustration. In the end it made me understand the other person more, why are they behaving like this, putting it in perspective and taking it at a pace that is more realistic and not in a 'muzungo' time frame instead of being upset.

Respondents' comments about cultural awareness suggest a far deeper process than one simply of observing and learning about different cultures. Indeed, what many volunteers learn, particularly if they are able to spend some time in one location and build relationships effectively with their peers, is that cultural awareness is more than about observing difference; it is fundamentally about trying (as a privileged outsider) to understand behaviour and engage with the contextual underpinnings of that. Greatrex-White (2008) argues that the experience of being a 'foreigner' is underrated, and that this 'disturbance' affects cultural knowledge and perspectives. The following volunteer explains that she has learnt that cultural awareness involves '*making less assumptions about what someone's behaviour says about their thoughts and feelings*'. This is where the distinction between shallow forms of 'voluntourism' (observation of difference) which may reinforce cultural stereotypes and actually working alongside colleagues in a very different environment lies. The final case cited here recounts the experience of a British Muslim doctor:

> I am more in tune with how cultural differences affect you professionally; you can't go in there and start shouting and screaming, you need to build relationships. I always knew they were important but maybe didn't appreciate how important. I will be a lot more in tune about how I'm making people feel because I've been in situations where all of a sudden I'm the foreigner.

The respondent goes on to identify some very specific scenarios where these skills could be actioned:

> The way I do consent will change. I will understand when an 80-year-old grandmother who's broken her hip and says, 'I want to wait for my son to arrive before I sign'. Oh gosh there's going to be a delay, why can't this 80-year-old just say yes? We are here for her benefit and she's delaying her own treatment. But now I think, 'actually you know what, you should wait for your son because it's important for you, whilst it's important for me to give you the right treatment as soon as possible, I can see that your priority is to wait here for your son to arrive'. So I think it will influence a whole area of things; cultural awareness, family awareness, how important family is to patients.

## TEACHING, RESEARCH AND PRESENTATIONAL SKILLS

There is some reference in existing research to the role that international placements play in terms of developing teaching, presentational and research skills (Banatvala and Macklow-Smith 1997; Lovett and Gidman 2011). Much of the literature regarding development of teaching skills refers to the experience of adapting existing skills to new environments, or having the opportunity to practice already established teaching skills (Jones et al. 2013). This is one component of learning that is very much a reflection of placement structure and volunteer roles and will be more evident in capacity-building interventions. Health Partnership projects, such as the SVP, funded by the Tropical Health Education Trust (THET) are focused on systems change through capacity-building. This has implied a heavy emphasis on knowledge transfer through CPD-style interventions (Ackers et al. 2016). The SVP has attempted to shift this emphasis from formal classroom style teaching/training to encourage mentoring on the job through co-working as our research indicates greater impact on behaviour change. In this respect SVP volunteers have been explicitly characterised as knowledge intermediaries and co-researchers/teachers. In practice this thrusts volunteers into a wide variety of (co) teaching roles and research activities including

- The development of classroom teaching skills including teaching to large and diverse multi-professional audiences
- Active engagement in the development of continuing professional development often involving protocol/guidance adaptation to local circumstances and associated training to promote implementation and behaviour change
- On-the-job mentoring and supervision, often across diverse multi-professional teams
- Presentation of their work to other volunteers, professionals and policy-makers/stakeholders
- Applying for grants and designing/costing projects.

The following nurse volunteer talked about her teaching experiences:

I was asked to teach medical students – formal teaching on the special care unit on respiratory management etc. Your confidence just goes up because these are people who are training to be doctors and save people's lives and they are seeking to learn from you. Now I know I have something to give; it gives me satisfaction.

In this case the volunteer engaged in a wide variety of knowledge transfer activities ranging from active mentoring of midwives and nurses on-the-job in a health facility, through organisation of intense CPD programmes in conjunction with a British paediatrician volunteer. She also organised the rotation of staff between facilities to optimise opportunities for learning and became involved in the formal class room teaching of medical students. It is clear from her narrative that she gained huge confidence from this. However, her interview in the UK suggested an immediate frustration as she was very aware that she would be unable to engage in these activities in her role in the NHS.

In the next case a UK obstetrician explains how the teaching components of her work stretched her previous teaching skills developing new areas of competency. It is important to note that in this context most of the clinical work in the hospital she was based in was undertaken by undergraduate nursing students on placement and medical interns (trainee doctors). In that sense she was working with health workers who are at a very active stage in their own learning:

> I've used some of my teaching skills, but I've realized teaching out here is so different to the UK and a lot of the skills I have for teaching in the UK aren't applicable here. It's quite hard to engage students out here in that way because they are not used to being taught in the way I do in the UK. So I've had to adapt a lot of my teaching skills. Practically, I've done quite a lot of operating, mostly with the interns (trainee doctors) and it's really helped me with my practical tutoring, most of the time in the UK I've been teaching relatively simply operations whereas here none of the operations are simple so I've been letting them do it and that means that when they get stuck they might have made a difficult situation very difficult so then its stretched my skills to get them out of that situation.

In another case involving a team of UK midwifery and nursing volunteers, the teaching roles formed a new and exciting component of their work that motivated her to explore new career directions:

> Teaching – I guess that's been the biggest part of my four months. And I just feel really positive about that. One thing that I have got out of the teaching in terms of my own career development is that I think I would really like to go in to teaching. I really really enjoyed the teaching and we ended up teaching over 200 midwifery students. They just want to know absolutely everything that they can get from you and you feel like they really listen and engage. So from my own perspective, I think that might be something I would consider further down the line. I know I won't be a midwife for the rest of my life, I wanna do other stuff within midwifery and I didn't know I'd want to do teaching. I always thought it was something I'd never ever want to do.

Depending on a range of factors, professional volunteers will also have unique opportunities to develop as researchers engaged in evidence-based interventions (Jones et al. 2013). In the SVP context this has involved multi-lateral processes of; harnessing volunteers to support research-based interventions (two volunteers were deployed as programme evaluators);

supporting volunteers' suggestions for research-based interventions and finally working in terms to develop research initiatives proposed by Ugandan colleagues. Of course teaching and research go hand-in-hand and all those volunteers engaged in teaching will have researched the topics they are working on:

> I have read up on things a lot. You have to read up well before you teach – you must know your topic. I was not doing formal teaching (in the UK) at all.

## SUMMARY

This chapter has reviewed the available research and empirical data collected during the SVP and MOVE projects to summarise the key areas of learning gained from professional volunteering in low-resource settings. There can be little dispute that such placements provide fertile and unique environments for professional development in areas that are of key concern to organisations such as the UK's National Health Service and explicitly recognised in current NHS training objectives. An important theme running through the learning theories literature and echoed in respondents' experiences suggests that the learning that happens in such international contexts is informal by nature with a much greater emphasis on tacit knowledge. Marsick and Watkins describe the *'incidental learning which occurs in institutions, as not typically classroom-based or highly structured, and where control of learning rests primarily in the hands of the learner'*. Learning in these environments becomes integrated with daily routines, is triggered by internal or external jolts; a haphazard, and inductive process of reflection and action linked to the learning of others (Marsick and Volpe 1999). Of course this is precisely what makes it difficult to measure. The following chapter moves on to consider some of the costs and potential risks associated with placements and approaches to mitigating risks and structuring placements so as to optimise relevant learning.

## NOTES

1. The second component of the MOVE project is focused on developing a psychometric tool to measure learning outcomes and will be reported separately.
2. www.knowledge4change.org.uk/our-projects
3. We are using the word culture here to refer to occupational culture.

4. This can be contrasted to the experiences of undergraduate mental health nurses who identified important areas of learning in relation to the side effects of drugs (Ahmed et al. 2016).
5. Positionality is defined by the Oxford English Dictionary as, 'The occupation or adoption of a particular position in relation to others, usually with reference to issues of culture, ethnicity, or gender'.

# CHAPTER 4

# Managing Costs and Risks

**Abstract** This chapter identifies some of the 'costs' associated with health worker placements in low-resource settings; it begins with a discussion of the costs of covering staff time during placements and some of the fears surrounding skills 'wastage' before highlighting risk areas associated with such placements.

**Keywords** Costs · Risks · Skills wastage · Measurement

## BACKGROUND: THE NHS IN FISCAL CRISIS?

On the basis of the research we have conducted and our experiential learning as managers of professional volunteering projects, we have no doubt that placements in low-resource settings both identify and invest in entrepreneurial knowledge and innovation. We also know that the remodelling of care in the current NHS environment in response to rising levels of chronic and complex conditions requires new forms of critical connective knowledge. Addicott et al. (2015) express the need for, 'closer attention to the role of generalists [in an environment] where care is delivered in teams based around the patient rather than in professional silos' (2015: 34). International placements deliver precisely this form of knowledge. But this learning, however valuable in its own right, is taking place in a specific economic, political and temporal context. The NHS is facing a financial crisis. And this is best characterised as a human resource crisis, as 70% of recurring costs relate to staffing (Addicott et al. 2015: 2). The 'crisis' is specifically manifest in an alarming growth in reliance upon temporary and agency staff. According to a recent document, NHS spending on agency staff has 'increased to the extent that it is one of the most significant causes of deteriorating Trust finances' (NHS Improvement Agency Rules 2016: 4). New rules designed to control this spend have introduced a cap (ceiling) on the level of pay that NHS employers can offer agency staff; in the case of junior doctors and other medical/clinical staff the cap is set at 55% above basic pay rates. The document explains how to cost agency staff using specified hourly rates and provides illustrative costs for a consultant doctor at £652.96 for an eight-hour shift. Based on these figures, providing staff cover or 'back-fill' for a junior doctor on an international placement for 12 months could cost around £66,760 (p. 20).[1] The Royal College of Nursing also produced a report on the 'unprecedented' reliance on agency nurses in the current 'perilous' financial crisis and projected an annual NHS spend of at least £980 million on agency nursing by the end of 2015 (RCN 2015: 3). This is the environment within which the MOVE project was tasked to weigh up the costs and benefits associated with professional volunteering.

The costs identified above concern only replacement salaries. What if the placements themselves generate new costs in relation to the individuals involved? Sherraden et al. (2008) suggest that the overwhelming majority of studies focus on the positive returns on professional volunteering with little attention paid to costs. In some ways, even personal experiences which are ostensibly (or actually) negative at the time can be regarded as having a positive effect in the long run. As we have noted, experiencing failure can stimulate innovation. However, there are, largely unsubstantiated, concerns that long periods overseas can result in elements of skills wastage, absorption within cultures of bad practice or desensitisation to risk. More specifically, there is a genuine risk that personnel may be exposed to infectious disease, terrorism, road traffic accidents and other forms of stress or trauma which generate new costs for the NHS. The systematic review conducted as part of the MOVE project identified a number of perceived 'externality' effects. These can be loosely grouped as follows:

1. Financial costs of staff replacement (as above)
2. Potential career risks (re-integration, negative attitudes of colleagues, professional revalidation)
3. Risk components (insurance, health and safety and security issues, personal trauma).

4. Cultural awareness
5. Personal impacts (loneliness, relationship tensions, fears of becoming judgemental on return)
6. Environmental impacts associated with air travel.

These concerns map onto the findings from the interviews with returned volunteers, although it must be said that the balance tips very strongly in the direction of benefits and these issues are typically mentioned only when respondents are encouraged to think in those terms. The following section discusses some of the issues raised.

## Professional Voluntarism and 'Brain Drain'

The most tangible and immediate risk to the NHS is for the placement experience to stimulate a desire for future mobility or eventual emigration. It is well established that early career or early life mobility tends to foster a desire or the confidence to engage in future mobilities (Ackers 2003; King and Ruiz-Gelices 2003). We have also identified a number of cases where individuals were motivated in the first instance to engage in professional voluntarism as an active decision to develop a career in global health. The following case is illustrative:

> I had an ulterior motive, I applied for MSF (Médecins Sans Frontières) a while ago and I didn't have enough management skills. I've worked in the humanitarian sector before but not with front line stuff.

The line manager in the following case suggests that some volunteers may find it difficult to return to the NHS and take the decision to engage in further international work once they return. She does suggest that it may not be the placement as such but the personality involved that precipitates this more 'footloose' approach to career planning:

> I think it is hard coz sometimes when they come back I think they don't fit here anymore and they leave again. Those with certain types of personality probably would have – its gonna happen anyway, but maybe it happens earlier [Line Manager]

In this and several other cases, the applicant was already planning to leave the NHS, at least temporarily, for a career in a low-resource setting or in global health more generally. In such situations, international placements provide important opportunities to take the first steps for leaving the NHS. In one case, the volunteer later signed up for a master's programme in global health; in another, a midwife left her position in the UK prior to departure with no intention to return immediately after her placement. Of course, these plans subsequently change and individuals may actually return to the NHS either immediately or in the future. In one case, a volunteer who took up a placement immediately after completion of a master's programme in global health and actively planned a career in global health at that stage in their career later returned to the UK to commence nurse training. Further down the line, he may elect to spend some time in a nursing capacity in a low-resource setting.

Having said that, in most cases where mobility creates an appetite for future work in low-resource settings this takes the form of an interest, often transformed into action, in getting involved in subsequent short stays (typically two weeks taken during vacations or study leave) perhaps to deliver specific training or 'virtual' engagement through mentoring of colleagues. The opportunities for individuals undertaking placements in low-resource settings to up and leave the NHS are very limited and restricted to those specifically interested in global health. On that basis, there is far less risk that they will leave to take more attractive positions or transition into long-term or settled forms of migration as the labour markets are simply not conducive to that. It would be rare to find professional employment in a low-resource setting that could even begin to sustain an employee let alone a family. In that respect, international placements in high-resource settings pose a much greater 'brain drain' risk. Recent interviews with British doctors and nurses in New Zealand identified a strong relationship between early career placements and future career decision-making facilitating the longer-term emigration of UK junior doctors.[2]

Career decision-making is increasingly boundaryless (Arthur 1994, 2014; Arthur and Rousseau 1996) and less likely to follow simple linear pathways and individuals change their perspectives over time. Whilst placement experiences may provide an opportunity to test the waters and potentially leave the NHS, they may also provide the impetus for a decision to return to it with renewed motivation:

> I was getting frustrated with the NHS cos I couldn't get away to volunteer. My Deanery were like, sorry [name]. Where I wanted to go wasn't recognised as a training placement as there were no senior medics there. I was

seeing colleagues who were going away for what was effectively a year in Australia and places like that. It's supposed to be training, but half the time it's sitting on Bondi Beach. Or they were doing management fellowships where they sit in an office for a year. But I was feeling like I wanted to do something that was actually useful to other people. I got very frustrated, so I decided I needed to resign and once I'd decided, it all sort of fell into place. I'm now back in the NHS, working as a locum registrar, but my intention is to get back into the NHS as a permanent registrar. I think I'm more committed now than before I left, but if I hadn't have left when I did, I might not have come back.

## SKILLS WASTAGE

The next issue raised with some regularity (but once again by a minority) concerns potential skills wastage. There is no hard evidence in existing research or in our own empirical work of actual skills waste on return. However, prior to return, many volunteers do experience some anxiety about their ability to slot back into the NHS environment with its rigid protocols, hierarchical structures and high-tech equipment. Once they have returned and reintegrated into the NHS workforce, they typically reflect on this as a momentary confidence issue due to the gap in their use of specific types of equipment. This concern links nicely to the ideas of deliberative practice discussed earlier suggesting that anyone who is not regularly using a skill may experience some decline in confidence. Anaesthetists were most likely to raise this issue:

> I'm definitely de-skilled in the high-tech side of things, which is what I expected beforehand. All this high-tech equipment like fibre optic intubations. Even Epidurals. But that doesn't worry me because once you get back into your normal practice we quickly pick that up. At home working fulltime two or three weeks you'll be back to normal.

The first comment, '*I'm definitely de-skilled*' is a little alarming but is immediately followed by the reassurance that this de-skilling is very short lived and may be more about confidence and perception than explicit skills. In another case, a midwife expressed some anxiety about water births:

> I've gone back to post-natal first, so I'm not going straight back into labour suite yet. I'm scared of water births strangely, but I know if I call for help it will be there.

In other cases, respondents talked about doing some prior reading to prepare themselves, perhaps building on research skills and a 'can do' attitude honed during their placement:

> There are things I will have to go back and read up like patient monitoring – we would never use that here because it's just too modern, but I think it will just take a day or so.

Chapter 3 discussed the benefits of multi-professional working and working at the boundaries of one's own profession. This was viewed as an important benefit by most volunteers and a key locus of new learning. However, a small number of volunteers also expressed some concerns about the impact of this on their subject-specific knowledge. In one case, a nurse who had been working in paediatrics in the UK applied for a placement involving work with neonates. Although she enjoyed the challenge of working in this rather new environment on a neonatal unit, she did begin to express a desire to work with older children which fell outside the scope of the project and articulated this in terms of a decline in her specialist skills:

> This was always going to be a bit of a challenge because I've not worked with neonates before and I feel like we're [now] going in more of a midwifery direction. I'm actually quite happy to do that for a week or so but I wouldn't fancy for long term.

The study also identified isolated perceptions of what can best be described as a lapse into bad practice or 'cutting corners'; interestingly these are always reported 'second-hand' about a third party. One volunteer described a situation she had observed where a nurse who had been away from the UK for two years (deployed through another organisation) had begun to adopt some of the bad practices of local staff in relation to routine patient monitoring and recording. Another British nurse expressed concern that her volunteer colleagues were lapsing into bad practice rather than encouraging best practice amongst their peers:

> It's ended up that even the white people are doing that now. You were talking about de-skilling – what we're doing is changing our ways to cope with theirs, to fit in with them and suit theirs. We're seeing more of that from the white people rather than the other way around.

This respondent was one of very few cases of volunteers who requested to return to the UK prematurely after four months of a six-month placement. She had found leaving her teenage children, as a single parent, very challenging and found it hard to cope with the level of what she saw as negligence on an overwhelmingly busy maternity unit. It is difficult to know whether the practices she refers to concern professional volunteers making some necessary adjustments to their working practices to meet the needs of the resource-constrained local environment and 'make do' but without any de-skilling taking place as such, or whether they were simply taking the easy option and losing their sense of professionalism. Our observational research would certainly indicate the former and suggest that there is little risk that staff would not adhere to protocols on their return, although many did not relish a return to the level of bureaucracy and form-filling associated with the NHS. The following doctor explains how he had to 'make do' but this represented a conscious and necessary response to the situation and not a preference or indication of laziness:

> In this country we're highly specialised and we have to learn how to use a lot of equipment. When people go over there that's stripped away and you're just working with the bare bones. It's your responsibility to make do with what you've got, and that's an eye opener for people but I don't think people like to work that way. They like the security of working within the NHS and having skilled people around them. It's a lot safer.

In the following case, an anaesthetist had only allowed herself one week on her return home to relocate to a new position. This situation is quite common amongst junior doctors who rotate annually and will be commencing an entirely new position on return. Nurses and midwives more usually return to their old position reducing overall dislocation. It is interesting to see how this doctor talks about her communication skills:

> How are you feeling about returning to the NHS?
> Nervous, I haven't got any downtime between coming back and starting my job. I'm working in a brand new city, a brand new hospital, new doctors and I don't have a car or a house. I only have a week from arriving home to starting my job. I feel like I'm out of practice in a lot of things; I haven't done any gynaecology out here, I'm out of sync with all the good normal

practice that we should be using. Even communicating, I had a friend come out to stay and she asked me why I was talking in a ridiculous voice; she said I was talking really slowly. You realise you adopt a way of speaking so people understand you better, so to go back it's going to be really hard to kick out of it and speak normally.

There was some concern that extended stays could result in disengagement with the latest evidence-based practice and technological advances. In the following case, the respondent refers to an American colleague who has organised periods of repatriation to enable her to keep up to the speed of the latest research and advances:

> One of the clinicians from the [US] group is going to be there for three to five years. Obviously that is going to have a huge impact on her clinical practice where you cannot do basic investigations and things are moving on, there are papers being published every week that she is missing out on so they have set it up for her that every three or four months she goes back and gets updated.

This may well be a matter of confidence and clinical practice rather than knowledge as such as most volunteers will be able to access published papers and gain quite significant research skills during placements. Indeed, from an ethnographic perspective, the volunteer house in Kampala had an atmosphere of research – of constantly discussing and researching conditions and potential interventions. This discussion took place on a 24/7 basis so much so that visitors and on rare occasions volunteers themselves had to extricate themselves to gain some reprieve.

The interviews, unsurprisingly, suggested a close relationship between the loss of confidence and length of stay. Longer stays tend to be associated with a greater decline in confidence in certain skills. On the other hand, this has to be balanced with the potential for skills gains in other areas which may derive from longer stays and, importantly, as this respondent points out, the relative benefits of the host setting:

> If you're coming for a month it's not worth it; you're only going to take. You won't be able to give that much in the space of a month – I've learnt and got so much out of it and really enjoyed it and just thought . . . the time has flown and that's the sign of a really positive experience. If people wanted to really do a lot of work I would struggle not to say, 'go for six months minimum.. a year or even better, two?

Do you think the longer the better?
  I do but there is a thing in that if you're out of the UK working or the US or the Western world of medicine are you deskilling yourself and are you as up to date and providing as good an obstetric advice as you could be? I've only been out four months, but I'm when I go back, I have a week of working with another midwife reorienting myself because I'm so out of the practice with writing notes and doing what we consider to be really top obstetric care…I need to re-familiarise myself with the speed at which I have to work at so I think if you're out for longer than a year you might lose a few skills…

One volunteer was faced with limited career options on return as her line managers had assumed a level of deskilling. Without any explicit consultation or communication, the decision was made to require her to work in the teaching hospital on her next rotation. At the time of interview this doctor was a little perplexed at the attitude of her employers and their implicit assumption that she posed something of risk especially as she had prepared herself for precisely that situation:

I didn't do foetal monitoring there. I think that is why they were concerned about me coming back so before I came back I made sure I refreshed my skills and stuff.

Asked whether she felt she had suffered from skills wastage and this had affected her practice on return, she replied: '*For me no, because I just think Uganda is different to the UK, I just adapt. You work to your environment. I just know it's a different system.*'
  An optional period of reintegration was subsequently built into the SVP program allowing one month on return when the volunteer could continue to receive their stipend and work on an unpaid basis. Experienced clinicians linked to the health partnerships and based in UK hospitals actively offered to mentor returned volunteers during this period. In practice, not one volunteer took up the offer.
  In Chapter 3, we referred to the distinction between explicit and tacit skills and the growing emphasis on what can perhaps best be called 'qualities' or professional attributes rather than skills. Tolerance is frequently cited as an example of attitudinal change brought about through placements in low-resource settings. However, respondents on some (relatively few) occasions suggested that their experiences of working in resource-constrained environments and witnessing the stoicism of these

patients may make them less tolerant of the more privileged patients in the UK. An experienced nurse with extensive experience in low-income settings highlighted an issue that many of our respondents mentioned:

> [when I came back] I had to be careful that I didn't judge people too much who chuntered about petty things. Because, you know, these complaints that patients and staff will make . . . I just stood there and I just thought, I really wanted to say this really isn't anything for you to complain about. You know, you want to be where I've just been and seen what I've seen.

## Exposure to Risk and Vicarious Liability

Risk is a major driver of policy and practice in large organisations such as the UK National Health Service. The systematic review identified a number of potentially negative impacts of international placements linked to risk, including insurance, litigation, health and safety, and security issues and personal trauma. As managers, our experience of managing and evaluating risk responsible for volunteer deployment, and more recently, the Ethical Electives Project, has emphasised the importance of distinguishing genuine and tangible risks from perceptions of risk. International placements in low-resource settings expose individuals and organisations to risk. Inflated, generalised or misguided perceptions of risks amongst potential volunteers, their families, line managers and policy makers add a further dimension generating obstacles to mobility (Ackers et al. 2014). Aversion to risk may damage learning and reduce opportunities for innovation.

The SVP commissioned a professional risk assessment undertaken by the Chief Risk Officer at the University Hospital of South Manchester NHS Foundation Trust (Paul Moore). In addition to his background in risk management within the NHS, Moore had also completed risk assessment on the ground in Uganda for the Man-Gulu Health Partnership. The risk assessment report describes risk management proactively as a process of anticipating the effect of uncertainty on the achievement of programme objectives and building resilience to mitigate that uncertainty (Moore et al. 2015). It distinguishes 'inherent' from 'residual' risk which is defined as 'the estimated level of risk exposure after taking additional steps to control (or mitigate) risk' (p. 8). Figure 4.1 presents the *inherent risks* identified, and Fig. 4.2 identifies the *residual risks* at the time of the

| Risk | Mean Score |
|---|---|
| Personal accident or injury including road traffic accident | 15.00 |
| Terrorist attack targeted at volunteers or project (suicide bomb, false imprisonment, kidnap or hostage) | 15.00 |
| Exposure to infection/tropical disease | 12.00 |
| Assault (verbal, physical, sexual) | 10.00 |
| Access to safe supply of food and drinking water at location | 10.00 |
| Lost (in unfamiliar and/or dark surroundings) | 10.00 |
| Needle stick injury (including provision of emergency HIV post-exposure prophylaxis) | 10.00 |
| Civil unrest/violent public disorder | 10.00 |
| Lone working | 6.25 |
| Slips, trips or falls on uneven, wet and/or muddy ground | 5.77 |
| Unsafe or unsupervised clinical activities | 5.25 |
| Sun exposure | 4.00 |

| VERY LOW RISK | | | LOW RISK | | | MEDIUM RISK | | | HIGH RISK | | | SIGNIFICANT RISK | | |
|---|---|---|---|---|---|---|---|---|---|---|---|---|---|---|
| 1 | 2 | 3 | 4 | 5 | 6 | 8 | 9 | | 10 | 12 | | 15 | 16 | 20 | 25 |

**Fig. 4.1**  Risks associated with professional voluntarism in clinical settings in Uganda

*Source*: Moore, Surgenor, Ackers-Johnson and Kakulgulu. (2015). SVP Risk Assessment. Available at: www.knowledge4change.org.uk/

| Hazard Profile | Overall Residual Risk Exposure (Taking Control Into Consideration) | | | | | | | | |
|---|---|---|---|---|---|---|---|---|---|
| | Kabubbu | Kasangati | Mulago | Fort Portal | Mbale | Hoima | Kisizi | Mbarara | Gulu |
| Access to safe supply of food and drinking water at location | 10 | 10 | 10 | 10 | 10 | 10 | 10 | 10 | 10 |
| Assault (verbal, physical, sexual) | 10 | 10 | 10 | 10 | 10 | 10 | 10 | 10 | 10 |
| Unsafe or unsupervised clinical activities | 3 | 9 | 15 | 3 | 3 | 3 | 3 | Unable to Evaluate | 3 |
| Civil unrest/violent public disorder | 10 | 10 | 10 | 10 | 10 | 10 | 10 | 10 | 10 |
| Exposure to infection/tropical disease | 12 | 12 | 12 | 12 | 12 | 12 | 12 | 12 | 12 |
| Lone working | 5 | 5 | 15 | 5 | 5 | 5 | 5 | Unable to Evaluate | 5 |
| Lost (in unfamiliar and/or dark surroundings) | 10 | 10 | 10 | 10 | 10 | 10 | 10 | 10 | 10 |
| Needle stick injury (including provision of emergency HIV post-exposure prophylaxis) | 10 | 10 | 10 | 10 | 10 | 10 | 10 | Unable to Evaluate | 10 |
| Personal accident or injury including road traffic accident | 15 | 15 | 15 | 15 | 15 | 15 | 15 | 15 | 15 |
| Slips, trips or falls on uneven, wet and/or muddy ground | 6 | 6 | 6 | 8 | 6 | 6 | 6 | 6 | 6 |
| Sun exposure | 4 | 4 | 4 | 4 | 4 | 4 | 4 | 4 | 4 |
| Terrorist attack targeted at volunteers or project (suicide bomb, false imprisonment, kidnap or hostage) | 15 | 15 | 15 | 15 | 15 | 15 | 15 | 15 | 15 |
| Are all risks acceptable (i.e. controlled as low as reasonably practicable (Y/N)? | Y | Y | N Co-presence & Lone working | Y | Y | Y | Y | N Unable to complete assessment | Y |

**Fig. 4.2** Residual risk exposure in placement locations

*Source*: Moore, Surgenor, Ackers-Johnson and Kakulgulu. (2015). SVP risk assessment. Available at: www.knowledge4change.org.uk/

initial risk assessment visit that was conducted prior to project commencement:

The judgement about whether identified risks are 'acceptable' or not in a particular context requires the relative balancing of risk 'severity' with risk 'likelihood.' On that basis risks associated with road traffic accidents or terrorism are graded as severe, although their likelihood may be low and mitigated by effective behaviour management. This process stimulated and informed the development of SVP volunteer management systems largely reflected in an evolving induction process and associated induction pack.[3] Over the past five years, the SVP has encountered most of the risks identified above. At the more alarming and less 'likely' end of the spectrum, there have been outbreaks of terrorism and civil disobedience (typically quite isolated and around election periods or involving tribal disputes). Road traffic accidents remain one of the greatest risks to volunteers in all low-resource settings (Gedde et al. 2011: 186). Bhatta et al. (2009) confirm the importance of road traffic accidents as a major cause of volunteer morbidity and mortality. In a survey of VSO volunteers, diarrhoea was the most prevalent heath risk reported (by 79.9%) with highest levels found amongst short stays and younger volunteers. This is followed by skin and dental problems and 17.5% reported some form of road traffic injury. The authors are clear to point out that the response rate to their survey was small (36%) and that this response rate may be skewed in favour of those who had experienced problems (and had something interesting to report). The situation is exacerbated in the Ugandan context by the use of 'boda bodas' (motorcycle taxis) and a study of Peace Corps volunteers in Africa found that 60% of road accidents were related to motorcycle use (Bernard et al. 1989). These risks to individuals also present a risk to the NHS potentially affecting the subsequent safe return of work-fit employees.

Exposure to infectious disease presents more direct potential impacts on return and these are risks that the wider public may become aware of and sensitised to.[4] Since the commencement of the SVP, Uganda has experienced at least three localised outbreaks of Ebola and Marburg haemorrhagic fever. We have also witnessed several instances of needle-stick injury. Both of these were responded to immediately triggering expert advice and a constant iteration of the induction pack.

Whilst NHS employers may be interested in the well-being of employees on placement, they are also anxious about the liabilities associated with that and the impact that any local incidents may have on volunteer's fitness to practice on return. This raises issues around clinical registration on placement and professional indemnity insurance.

All of these risks can be mitigated to some extent through attentive volunteer management supported by active relationships on the ground. It may provide some reassurance to readers to point out that over the past five years we have deployed well over 60 long-term professional volunteers and 110 undergraduate students in Uganda without any serious adverse outcomes.

One area highlighted in the risk assessment that is often overlooked and compounds all of the risks referred to above is that of lone or unsupervised working. We have discussed some of the implications of supervision in relation to optimal learning outcomes (Chapter 3). In some situations it could be argued that lone working or working without close supervision generates profound opportunities for innovative learning especially for more senior volunteers. International placements certainly attract individual clinicians keen to work outside the perceived constraints of NHS structures. The risk assessor described volunteering in low-resource settings as a 'magnet for mavericks' during initial discussions about risk and this is certainly confirmed by our experiences of recruiting and subsequently managing volunteers, especially doctors and more senior doctors some of whom actively seek out opportunities for what one junior doctor termed 'ninja medicine'.

Managing volunteer–health worker relationships has formed a major focus of the SVP process leading to the operationalisation of rigorous systems to prevent lone working for all cadres of staff. Drawing on previous research on highly skilled migration and knowledge mobilisation we have imported and operationalised the concept of 'co-presence.'[5] Co-presence is a necessary (but not sufficient) condition for mutual learning and reduces the risks associated with gap-filling and labour substitution (Ackers and Ackers-Johnson 2014). It is also a key component of risk mitigation. At one level, it links to other health risks, such as needle stick injury where policy requires that the individual must seek immediate HIV prophylaxis. It is also a key component of managing litigation or more commonly in many low-resource settings, the impact of blame cultures. In this environment, having witnesses is of critical importance. At another, more complex level, it requires and assists professional volunteers to manage the daily pressures on them to perform out with their competency.

Many medical and nursing students and junior doctors in low-resource settings are required to work without supervision often running services on their own (Ackers et al. 2016). This environment puts huge pressure on UK volunteers to do likewise. This 'expectation' and peer pressure is further compounded by irresponsible international organisations that place volunteers in gap-filling roles without adequate supervision or support. The risk assessment visit identified a shocking example of this, involving British medical students encouraged by their 'virtual' UK clinical supervisor to work at nights for data collection purposes:

> Medical students explained how they were often goaded into carrying out clinical examination or diagnostic procedures they did not feel competent to perform, and whilst they declined to carry out the procedures, they explained how this created some tension with Ugandan medical students also working at the Hospital (Moore et al. 2015: 15)

Concerns about lone working and the complexities of establishing rules that were suitable to a wide range of volunteers from different professions, levels of seniority and personal competence/confidence led to the co-development of the 'SVP Competency Algorithm.'[6] This was developed as a flexible working guide to empower volunteer decision-making when confronted with lone working or lack of effective supervision.

The case cited above involved students and UK volunteers who were working at night. The risks associated with lone working are elevated during night time and weekend working. A simple response to this is to prevent volunteers from working during these times and ensure that local staff are aware that this 'rule' is imposed by the deploying organisation rather than a simple volunteer preference. The issue of working hours is also present in some volunteer interviews. In keeping with the spirit of UK law the SVP instituted strict policies on working hours to prevent over working and the risks of exhaustion and trauma arising from that. The general lack of adherence to timetables in Uganda and many other low-resource settings can place pressure on those staff who are committed to their work to work extremely long hours to cover for absenteeism and poor time management. In most cases it is concerns about patients and leaving wards unattended that encourages long working hours. However, some volunteers based in mission hospital facilities faced undue pressure from British managers to commit to arduous working schedules that would not be permitted in the UK and subjected to humiliation if they questioned this. Weekly reporting mechanisms and close relationships with volunteer managers enabled us to support volunteers in these circumstances and to relocate volunteer to other Health Partnerships if situations did not improve.[7]

The research has identified a number of other areas of concern which have the potential to cause stress to professional volunteers. In many ways these sit hand-in-hand with key areas of learning underlining our contention that some of the most acute learning arises from discomfort. Whilst positive learning may indeed accrue, it is important that professional volunteers are protected and supported. The first of the areas concerns experiences of overt discrimination. The most prevalent form of discrimination identified involves attitudes towards women. A mid-career anaesthetist describes her experience:

> I have come up against fairly misogynistic attitudes and several misunderstandings about whether or not I am actually a doctor. In fact, I am fairly certain on one occasion my ability or qualifications for teaching on the neo natal resuscitation course were questioned.

The following volunteer had six years specialist experience:

> People here think that I am younger than I am definitely, but my personal perception of the relationship that I have with [in-charge doctor] is that he does not take me particularly seriously. I thought maybe that was gender. I constantly had to prove myself but at the same time when the department had no doctors he was more than happy for me to go on the rota [alone] and do ward rounds.

Gender emerges with some regularity in volunteer narratives in the SVP. This reflects the feminised nature of employment in maternal health and the stronger tendency for women to volunteer (Hudson and Inkson 2006: Bhatta et al. 2009). The strongly hierarchical nature of professions and organisations in many low-resource settings generates a high potential for gender-based discrimination. This should not be confused with the more composite concept of 'culture/religion' that often conveniently obscures gender/human rights dynamics. The SVP project with its emphasis on maternal and new-born health was strongly skewed in favour of female volunteers (Table 4.1).

Most of the female doctors deployed within the frame of the SVP reported experiencing patronising behaviour from senior peers and managers. In many cases this manifests itself in stereotypical assumptions

**Table 4.1**   VP volunteers by gender

| | | |
|---|---|---|
| Anaesthetists | 10 (6 female) | 71 |
| Obstetricians | 9 (7 female) | 60 |
| Midwives | 8 (8 female) | 60 |
| Nurses | 6 (6 female) | 48 |
| Foundation year 2 doctors | 4 (2 female) | 30 |
| Paediatricians | 3 (0 female) | 33 |
| Social scientists | 2 (1 female) | 24 |
| Biomedical engineers | 1 (0 female) | 26 |
| General practitioners | 1 (1 female) | 6 |
| **Total** | **44 (31 female)** | **358** |

*Source*: SVP Final Report, 2014.

about their appearance and how 'young' (read inexperienced) they looked. In one case, where the author herself was present in a meeting with a representative of the Ministry of Health, the (male) turned to the obstetrician and asked her if she was a medical student. In response to a gentle assertion that she was a qualified obstetrician he replied that she 'looked much younger'. Another volunteer refers to the difficult relationship she had with her Ugandan line manager whom she felt did not treat her as an equal and take her seriously. Concerned about this she spoke to her predecessor (a male volunteer at the same level of seniority and discipline), *'he said the head of department was always fine with him. It sounded like it was much easier for him. I did not feel being a woman [was easy] in an environment like Uganda, even though women are able to be doctors'*.

Two anaesthetic volunteers at the same level of seniority discussed the impact of gender on their relationships with local staff:

[Female volunteer] I think it's harder, harder for women.

[Male volunteer] Yep, definitely.

[Female] Without a shadow of a doubt. I think you've got to understand the society you work in, so I think being female, I wouldn't say being male is an advantage, but I would say being female is a disadvantage. Traditionally their culture in some of the tribes. You're coming into that, and then you're asking men in their fifties and sixties to listen to a young, white female (volunteer) that's a tall order in a hierarchical patriarchal society. My very first day, and I don't harp on about this, the principal [clinician] physically pushed me out of his way. Not in any forceful way, but it was definite.

A mid-career obstetrician illustrates the inter-section of different dimensions of 'positionality' and the impact on learning and behaviour change:

> Over the last week alone I must have said at least 40 times, 'don't suction the baby when it's breathing and crying', 'stop suctioning', 'please stop', 'can you put the suction down'. It's just really hard, when it's so engrained in what they do for some white person to come along and say 'no'. The working relationships I have with most of the midwives are good. They often just see me as another pair of hands, as marginally more competent than their junior doctors. They don't completely believe me in certain things but they tolerate me because they know I'll come in and do some c sections. The interns (doctors in training), I did have quite good relationships with. But one of them I'm not getting on with, he's being directly challenging towards me. He will challenge me on pretty much everything I say, and I'm sure it's because I'm white and female and he doesn't understand me.

Attitudes about gender are often intertwined with professional boundaries and hierarchies compounded by gender segregation; all midwives and nearly all nurses are female in Uganda. Another 'twist' on the disciplinary aspects of positionality emerges in multidisciplinary interventions. An experienced volunteer midwife explains her treatment by a local doctor during a multidisciplinary 'Well Woman' intervention:

> We had a local doctor that spoke to me absolutely appallingly like, 'get this', 'do this', 'do the other'.

Professional hierarchies are by no means a feature only of Ugandan health systems. Indeed, some of the most valuable transferable skills gained by professional volunteers are connected to experiences of multidisciplinary team working. These hierarchies are often rarefied in low-resource contexts with firm boundaries obstructing effective cross-professional cooperation and team working. Another area that poses a challenge to professional volunteers concerns their treatment as 'outsiders'. We have noted above how this may stimulate active and effective learning around cultural awareness. On the other hand, it can amount to forms of quite explicit and distressing stereotyping.

## CULTURE AND 'RACIAL' STEREOTYPING

Although translated strictly to mean 'white', the concept of 'mzungu' in Africa[8] refers in more complex ways to 'wealthy' foreigners. It is also linked to an historic association of professional voluntarism with mission-ary-style, 'donor-recipient' voluntarism. An example of this can be seen in the nickname given to one volunteer as 'Dr Donor'. In many instances volunteers are viewed as 'cash cows' rather than co-workers. This percep-tion of volunteer roles reinforces the expectation that volunteers come to low-resource settings as locums and donors challenging the commitment to knowledge exchange and co-presence. A good example of this is the caricature of clinicians in low-resource settings as the passive recipients of training at the opposite pole on a linear knowledge gradient; as individuals lacking capabilities and collectively, the system lacking experienced per-sonnel.[9] These myths continue to shape development interventions dama-ging relationships and limiting impact. They create obstacles to the achievement of the kinds of balanced professional relationships experi-enced in other international contexts based on collegiality.

The stereotypes associated with the 'mzungu' concept are tainted with misunderstandings about experience, skills, seniority and relative wealth. We noted above how female volunteers tend to be viewed as 'young' by senior Ugandans. In other situations, 'mzungus' are perceived by their peers as more experienced and possessing higher skills. This can place British trainees in positions where their competency is stretched (as noted above). It can also cause distress to professional volunteers.

The 'fluffy' concept of culture tends to gloss over or even excuse discrimi-natory and unprofessional behaviour. This narrative from an early career obstetrician shows how this stereotyping of UK volunteers can put them at risk especially when, as in this case, they are working in isolation at night:

> We arrived at 8 pm. From the start midwives were sleeping in the office. The doctors worked until 3am when they all went to sleep and said that they would be up at 6am. The theatre staff all stopped work at 3am and went to sleep, despite there being women waiting for caesareans. During this time anything could have happened. I was delivering one baby after another often on the floor in the waiting area and dealing with complex obstetric emer-gencies. A woman died which was emotionally draining. There was an off-duty security guard taking bribes off patients and moving them to the labour ward. Then I had the doctor go mad at me for documenting in the notes

that the reason I couldn't take a woman to theatre was because they were all asleep (despite waking them all up and informing them). He shouted at me in front of patients and staff. He showed them the notes I had written and accused me of trying to get them sacked justifying it by saying 'this is what happens in Uganda every night shift. We aren't in the UK now'. I felt vulnerable and didn't know how to get senior help. Being a mzungu in these working environments can be hard as no one really wants to help you if it interferes with their routine.

## AVOIDING RISKS THROUGH INTERNATIONAL PLACEMENTS IN HIGH-RESOURCE SETTINGS?

The discussion above has identified a range of potential costs, risks or 'disbenefits' associated with placing NHS employees in low-resource settings. It is important to reiterate that, from the perspectives of respondents and our experiences as volunteer managers, the gains far outweigh the costs. In practice, we have seen very few examples of these risks converting into serious outcomes. It could be argued that people do not need to travel to such extreme locations, with all the expense and general upheaval that this involves, in order to be exposed to difficult working conditions. Apart from activities that might be specifically tied to the location, the UK could arguably provide plenty of environments in which to develop the skills that are claimed to be uniquely fostered in low-income settings (McCulloch and Mishra 2009; Yule et al. 2006). However, although the UK, or any high-income country, may have some extremely deprived socio-cultural areas, anyone who has travelled or worked in low-resource settings will acknowledge that what can be experienced in such places is fundamentally different. Poverty and systemic dislocation in the UK in no way approach the levels that can be found in parts of the developing world. We asked the managers of volunteering organisations that currently provide overseas placement opportunities to comment on the difference between sending staff to high- and low-income countries. A senior coordinator with several years' experience of organising long term placements for health professionals was clear about the situation as she saw it:

> I'm not absolutely sure they get that much out of going to high resource settings. I think it's completely different. I think that clinical staff may get a bit of training in comparative systems, but they'll have the same restrictions

that affect them here. The problem in the UK is that they don't get their hands on any complex cases, like twin or breech deliveries, because of litigation and defensive practice. Because of the sheer weight of trainees, I guess, they will see so few of the cases that they need to see to progress. So when they go to a developing country they get so much more hands on. They might do observation – they might be able to observe over here, but they'll see things that they've read about in text books that over here aren't allowed to mature onto real problems – like ruptured uteruses, or diabetic foot ulcers.

Volunteers themselves who had experienced working in both high- and low-income settings highlighted similar issues. There was a general feeling that working in any foreign setting, be it low- or high-income, would be valuable and support a degree of 'systems thinking'. Even comparatively similar high-resource settings such as America or Australia, where elements such as a shared language helped to mitigate excessive culture shock, were seen as worthwhile, although it was usually acknowledged that they tended not to offer the experiential onslaught that is a feature of low-resource settings. Bethany, a recently qualified nurse who had already undertaken long-term placements in Central Africa, Tanzania and Australia, explained how the differences between the Australian and the UK high-income settings were largely administrative. The Australian healthcare system is a form of hybrid public/private arrangement which she found very easy to adjust to. It engendered none of the shock value which characterised her low-resource placements:

> I think it's always good to go to somewhere different to experience something else. I think as much as it's a nice idea to stay in one job once you've qualified, I don't necessarily think it's a good idea because you don't know anything different. [In Australia] it was the same sort of culture, pretty much. Some things I'd be like, 'do you not do it like this?', and they'd say 'no' but it's just little differences. Main procedures and stuff pretty much all the same. The hospital set-ups and the hierarchies are very much the same.

A meeting with UK midwives in Australia suggested that, from a midwifery perspective, the work in Australia was less challenging than their previous work in the UK, as midwives had less autonomy in that setting. This can be contrasted with the situation described by midwives in New Zealand which has witnessed a marked policy shift in favour of independent midwives practicing with a very high degree of autonomy.[10]

Disengaging with the system one is familiar with facilitates a level of (comparative) systems-thinking that health professionals are less likely to engage in in the absence of mobility. The MOVE project did not set out to explicitly compare experiences in high- and low-resource settings and future research may prove highly valuable particularly if it is able to address experiences in areas such as the remote Australian outback. For now, we can conclude that placements in high-resource settings are less likely to present the opportunities for clinical practice or leadership that are associated with low-resource settings, and they are far more likely to act as a precursor to longer-term stays and potential settlement given the relative attractiveness of positions.

## Summary

This chapter has rehearsed some of the potential externality effects of international placements in low-resource settings. The most important of these concerns the financial costs of providing staff cover for NHS employees in the current human resource crisis. In addition to this, there are risks associated with such placements and it is essential that they are exposed and discussed. In practice, the perception of risk is a far greater barrier to placements than actual or inherent risks often exacerbated by forms of moral panic and lack of contextual knowledge. Risk mitigation through effective project organisation and volunteer management can significantly reduce residual risks and balance the relationship between risk management and optimal learning.

The final chapter summarises the discussion presented so far and concludes with a presentation of the Volunteer Deployment Model developed and continually refined in the course of the Sustainable Volunteering Project.

## Notes

1. This is without taking into account any costs associated with the volunteer such as pensions.
2. A pilot study was completed in August 2015 and further work is planned.
3. The SVP also provides every volunteer with 'Working in International Health' (Gedde et al. 2011).

4. https://www.theguardian.com/world/2016/aug/18/pauline-cafferkey-ebola-nurse-accused-concealing-high-temperature
5. Understanding 'Co-Presence' in the Sustainable Volunteering Project, Policy Report 2014 available at www.knowledgeforchange.org.uk/
6. The tool was designed by Drs Kim McCloud and Helen Schofield and is reproduced in Ackers, Lewis and Ackers-Johnson (2014).
7. Our sister book (Ackers-Johnson 2014) has a specific recommendation aimed at such organisations to make registration with UK Charities Commission contingent upon compliance with mainstream UK policy and practice in employment and equality matters.
8. According to Wikipedia, 'mzungu' is a Bantu language term used in the African Great Lakes region to refer to people of European descent. It is a commonly used expression among Bantu peoples in Kenya, Tanzania, Malawi, Rwanda, Burundi, Uganda, Democratic Republic of Congo and Zambia, dating back to the eighteenth century. Strictly defined as an 'aimless wanderer', the term is used in Uganda to refer generically to non-African 'outsiders' – usually but not always white people.
9. A point we discuss in our sister volume (Ackers-Johnson 2014).
10. These interviews were organised as part of a scoping visit to New Zealand and a conference visit to Perth, Australia; see note 2 above.

# Conclusions: Towards a Model for Sustainable Professional Volunteering

**Abstract** Chapter 5 presents a brief summary of key issues. Returning to the conceptualisation of professional volunteers as knowledge intermediaries, it emphasises the critical learning opportunities associated with placements in low-resource settings. It then cautions against equating mobility metrics with notions of excellence per se, arguing that any experience must be judged on its outcomes if we are to preserve principles of equality of opportunity in National Health Service (NHS) careers. It then presents the Sustainable Volunteering Model as the basis for future evidence-based up-scaling that complies with highest ethical principles whilst respecting the duty of care to professional volunteers.

**Keywords** Sustainability · Ethical deployment · Volunteer placements model

### Introduction: Professional Volunteers as Knowledge Brokers

Our previous work has characterised professional volunteers on international placements as 'knowledge brokers' engaged in forms of collaborative knowledge generation and mobilisation (Ackers 2015). Ongoing evaluation substantiated through the MOVE project has underlined the resonance of this conceptualisation. Extracting individuals from this process and attempting to distinguish volunteer learning and the returns to sending organisations such

© The Author(s) 2017
H.L. Ackers et al., *Healthcare, Frugal Innovation, and Professional Voluntarism*, DOI 10.1007/978-3-319-48366-5_5

as the NHS, whilst necessary, is also highly problematic both from a 'measurement' and an ethical perspective. The introduction to this book made a somewhat arbitrary distinction between explicit clinical skills and tacit knowledge. We identified the growing emphasis attached to tacit knowledge and 'transferable' or soft skills in NHS staff development priorities and, in Chapter 3, evidenced the impact that international placements have on these areas of learning. In reality, hard and fast distinctions between explicit and tacit knowledge break down as tacit knowledge is increasingly associated with all skills implementation. Williams and Baláž contend that these diverse forms of learning operate in combinations to bring about innovative thinking and behaviour change criticising the tendency to view skills in isolation as technical competences or, 'something that can be taught and assessed'. Meusberger (2009) makes a similar point, distinguishing knowledge from 'information'. The work of these authors recognises the importance of more socially situated and socially constructed forms of tacit knowledge to knowledge translation process. When it comes to understanding not simply whether new knowledge or skills are generated but more importantly whether these can be utilised in either the low-resource setting or the NHS on return, the distinction between forms of explicit and tacit knowledge loses significance; they are 'essentially complementary... because all forms of codified knowledge require tacit knowledge in order to be useful' (Meusberger 2009: 31).

We have seen how repetition of clinical skills on international placements not only hones skills but also builds the confidence required for skills utilisation. Similarly, whilst triage, audit or management skills can be taught, in theory, it is the experience of actioning these skills in dynamic cultural and political contexts that generates higher-level experiential learning and opportunities for knowledge translation and implementation in future environments. The UKs Medical Research Council highlights the increasing importance of 'complex interventions' to the contemporary NHS (MRC 2008; Richards et al. 2015). The multi-professional experiential learning that takes place on international placements provides opportunities for the kind of systems thinking so important to complex interventions. It enables individuals to step outside of their immediate position and view organisations more holistically from the outside.

Chapter 1 discussed the use of the word 'volunteer' in global health research and policy arguing that although the term captures a factual legal situation (that they are not employees in the host locations), it fails to convey the reality of individual motivations and learning. The prefix 'professional' was added to emphasise the essentially professional quality of these forms of highly skilled mobility as 'embodied knowledge' (Williams and Baláž 2008). We used the language of lifelong learning to break away from conventional stereotypes tying knowledge transfer processes to career stages; learning and teaching occur simultaneously across all stages of a professional career and life-course. This approach enables us to understand the contribution of even very early career health workers (or students) to low-resource settings and the learning opportunities for even the most senior of cadres. The concept of knowledge brokerage captures these processes perfectly by placing health workers as critical knowledge intermediaries both during their placements and on their return to the NHS. Exposure to new learning combined with existing knowledge creates significant innovation potential. Sadly, host organisations and systems in low resource settings often fail to create environments receptive to this new knowledge. We have discussed these processes and the unintended consequences of professional voluntarism elsewhere (Ackers and Ackers-Johnson 2016). The MOVE project was tasked to capture the volunteer learning associated with international placements and the conditions for its optimisation. As a project, we were not instructed to assess the impact of that knowledge premium or the potential for knowledge translation and behaviour change within the NHS. Our interviews with returned volunteers would suggest that further work needs to be done to ensure that the NHS is more receptive to this knowledge if we are to realise the potential benefits associated with frugal innovation.

The knowledge, networking and mobility capital that professional volunteers gain as a result of their sojourns represents huge potential for the NHS. It also augments individuals' CVs in a way that adds to their 'employability security' (Opengart 2002) insuring them against the risk of dependency on any one employer and opening up opportunities across diverse sectors and countries. The growth of 'portfolio careers' increases opportunities for creativity and agency. The interviews have identified a number of cases where individuals have used their placements to re-imagine their careers and perhaps move out of the NHS into other health systems or other forms of work. Some actively chose professions such as medicine and nursing to pursue careers in global health; others became interested in global health or development work as a direct result of their exposure. The majority renewed their motivation to return to the NHS and use their new skills and confidence to stimulate innovation. Ultimately it is for the NHS to find ways of harnessing these qualities and energies to enhance the UKs National Health Service.

The remaining section of this chapter addresses some of the more operational aspects that need to be addressed if international placements are to be developed as a wider lifelong learning 'offer' accessible to all NHS employees rather than simply providing enhancements to the CVs of more privileged doctors.

## MOBILITY 'METRICS' AND EQUALITY ISSUES

In Chapter 1 we referred to the notion that professional mobility is a selective process and that mobile professionals are often identified as sitting amongst the 'brightest and the best'. Ferro (2006) suggests that mobility can take on a symbolic quality (or rite of passage) reflecting social norms as much as genuine ability or potential. Mobility, she argues, contributes to a 'self-actualisation process' that could be achieved through other mechanisms including forms of virtual connectedness. This work is of importance to the MOVE objectives (of presenting an evidence-based model for professional voluntarism) for two reasons. First, whilst mobility is clearly one means of achieving accelerated and enhanced learning, it is not the only way and it is critically important that health workers who have experienced international placements are evaluated according to the experiences and learning they have gained and not from the 'fact' of their involvement alone. International placements in low-resource settings are unlikely to generate consistent and comprehensive skills sets as such as every context and deployment is quite distinct. A study of doctoral mobility in the social sciences warned of the consequences of treating mobility as an indicator (or metric) of 'excellence' and concluded that 'mobility is not an outcome in its own right and must not be treated as such (as an implicit indicator of internationalisation). To do so contributes to differential opportunity in scientific labour markets reducing both efficiency and equality. Mobility is one means of achieving international research collaboration and knowledge transfer. It is not an end in itself' (Ackers 2008).[1] We would argue that the same applies to international placements and their role in the development of health professionals. Any automatic association (or presumed correlation) between placement mobility and notions of excellence could generate forms of discrimination privileging those in a position to access opportunities. Secondly, and linked to this, it is of utmost importance that we acknowledge the fact that health workers are not equally footloose and able to respond to mobility opportunities. Family and caring responsibilities and financial status as well as the attitudes of employers and line managers will have a significant effect on their ability to action any aspirations they have towards mobility (Ackers 2008, 2010; Boyd 1989). These processes are gendered and impact differently across the life course. Lifelong learning and its counterpart, the 'boundaryless career', will shape in important ways individuals' abilities to engage in international placements. Whilst finance alone will rarely be the only factor impeding mobility, the Sustainable Volunteering Project (SVP) certainly found that less well-remunerated cadres of staff such as nurses and midwives were more reliant upon compensatory payments to facilitate their engagement in international placements in comparison to doctors most of whom either have access to immediate resource or the ability to forgo income in the expectation of deferred gratification.

This issue of equality of opportunity will grow in significance if international placements become more of an expectation across all cadres of staff. At the present time it is primarily evident in relation to medical trainees where the expectation of mobility has existed for some time. Widening participation programmes will increase the potential for inequity in medicine as will the introduction of tuition fees for nursing, midwifery and allied health professions.[2] The survey results presented in Chapter 2 suggest that women are less likely to exercise these forms of mobility during the years associated with child bearing and rearing. These will often coincide with periods of accelerated career progression for their male counterparts. Consideration needs to be given to the barriers to engagement in international placements and the implications of these in terms of equality of opportunity. Promoting the view that international placements provide unique and career-enhancing opportunities will necessarily increase the demand for such placements and the kudos attached to this experience. The potential for opportunities to generate inequalities will be linked to, amongst other factors, length of stay and the perceptions of learning outcomes associated with this variable.

## LENGTH OF STAY ON INTERNATIONAL PLACEMENTS

The general consensus, at least among theorists of highly skilled migration, would seem to be that the distinction between short- and long-term stays holds little validity and may indeed constrain our understanding of learning (Ackers and Gill 2008; Iredale 2001). When discussing potential

stays with professional volunteers, the issue of length of stay usually forms
the basis of the first enquiry; 'How long do I have to stay for?' Length of
stay is also identified as a key issue for the host setting where conventional
wisdom and the practices of dominant deploying organisations (such as
VSO) have favoured extended stays (of over two years).[3] Our own evaluation of the relationship between length of stay and host impact informed
by contemporary research on highly skilled mobilities and business travel
provides a powerful critique of this perspective arguing that length of stay
is only one of a number of key variables impacting knowledge mobilisation
processes (Ackers 2015). Length of stay in isolation tells us nothing about
learning or impact.

In considering optimal models, we start from the premise that some
element of co-presence (physical meeting) is critical to relationship-building and the formation of effective inter-organisational interventions
(Williams and Baláž 2008; Meusberger 2009). The Tropical Health and
Education Trust (THET) recognise this in their scoping visit funding
stream enabling interested parties to meet and develop plans. The formation of strong relationships is critical not only to host impact but also to all
forms of bi-lateral learning, including volunteer placements. Stays for the
purpose of project initiation and development can be quite short and
intense and need to involve those individuals central to programme organisation.[4] The continued development of inter-institutional links can be
maintained through regular short stays; indeed, repeated (return) or cycli-
cal stays have a powerful symbolic and practical impact in maintaining
relationships and an up-to-date understanding of contextual dynamics.
Shrum et al. made a similar point in the context of understanding project
failure and corruption in Ghana arguing that strong and effective relationships are 'built through repeated visits over time' (2010: 161). Our paper
describes another type of stay focused specifically on knowledge mobilisation objectives at organisational as well as individual level. 'Long-term
volunteers' (defined by THET as stays involving a minimum of six
months) play a critical 'anchoring' function (Ackers 2015: 140) providing
continuity and communication in environments where virtual methods
(email etc.) are rarely optimal. These long-term volunteers play a key role
in maintaining organisational relationships and communication channels;
they also support those volunteers who are unable to stay for longer
periods to engage effectively in knowledge mobilisation roles and bi-lateral
learning. In the context of established and active health partnerships
stimulated and reinvigorated through repeat short stays and underpinned

by long-term anchoring volunteers, short stays focused on targeted inter-ventions can prove to be highly effective. Although our own survey did not identify a high incidence of repeat stays, our experience of working within the frame of the Ugandan Maternal and Newborn Hub provides numerous examples of repeat short stay visits especially amongst more senior clinicians. This is borne out by Smith et al.'s study (2012) which found that 33% of doctors on international placements of less than a month had returned on at least five occasions. Other literature supports the contention that short stays are conducive to volunteer learning (Dean 2013; Dowell et al. 2014; Dowell and Merrylees 2009; Smith 2012).

Long stays in the absence of active health partnerships run the risk of lapsing into service delivery often involving lone working and 'fly-in-fly-out' random short stays deliver little for host settings or volunteers. The exception to this may be emergency relief work, although even in these circumstances this must take place within the frame of credible and effec-tive organisational relationships. Organisations like the 'Mercy Ships'[5], for example, may provide effective opportunities for intense clinical learning on the part of short term and relatively junior health workers.

From the perspective of volunteer learning, length of stay is fundamen-tally about personal objectives and tailored volunteer deployment. Ackers (2015) argues that there is no ideal length of stay:

> The experience of short-term clinical exchanges in Health Partnerships suggests that where the visits are well organised, prepared for in advance and form an integrated component of a mutually planned and coordinated project, they can play a very important role in promoting knowledge trans-fer. The existence of clear (negotiated) project objectives (and annual prio-rities) tightens the focus, promoting continuity of the knowledge transfer activity. (Ackers 2015: 143)

On the basis of our contextualised experience we would disagree with Williams and Baláž's assertion that three-month stays represent a 'mini-mum for significant and effective learning' (2008: 1927). However, short stays have cost and management implications. A consultant anaesthetist volunteer describes the importance of having effective management sys-tems in place particularly for short-term volunteers:

> They've got to be managed very well. Any placement has got to be managed well but I think it's more important with a short-term placement. You need to make sure that you don't force in someone who's used to having a lot of

support. Here in the UK we have a very hierarchical structure – even a consultant can always get a second opinion on something. Even if people [criticise] the NHS, you'll never be on your own, even as a consultant. You can always ring up your director and say 'I'm really in [trouble] here, what would you do?' But then you've got to make sure that if you're a relatively junior person and you're going into an environment where you're not supported, then you've got to make sure that it's not going to be catastrophic. I mean, you get disasters [overseas] that you don't see in the UK, so you've got to make sure that there's some kind of network, some kind of infrastructure in place that's able to rescue them, protect them, whatever you want to call it. Which is going to be difficult. It'd be dreadful if a young doctor went out there who was really eager, really keen, and they end up in a situation where they want to go for help, but no help arrives cos there is no help there.

We have presented this quote in some detail as it leads naturally into the final section of the book which sets out the Sustainable Volunteering Model. We present this model here not as an example of 'best practice' but rather as guidance to aid potential policy transfer. Policy transfer is a complex process and it is never possible to pluck one model out of its context and attempt to transpose it into another quite different environment (Park et al. 2014, 2016). To echo the language of learning theories, the translation and operationalisation of this 'model' to another setting requires a further layer of knowledge brokerage by a 'knowledgeable other' (individuals or organisations with deeply contextualised knowledge of the local hosting environment). Strachan et al. make a similar point:

> Placement structures may not transfer appropriately, and there will certainly be new patterns of negotiation, organisation, strategy and management to learn, as well as new relationships to build and new needs to engage with. (2009: 12)

## TOWARDS A MODEL FOR SUSTAINABLE PROFESSIONAL VOLUNTEERING

### Sustainable and Ethical Deployment

First and foremost, professional volunteering needs to comply with ethical standards; the primary concern here is commitment to reciprocity and mutual benefit. This balance can be illustrated by reference to the original

SVP objectives which themselves echo the objectives of our funding body the Tropical Health and Education Trust and its funding, body, UK Aid:

1. To support evidence-based, holistic and sustainable systems change through improved knowledge transfer, translation and impact.
2. To promote a more effective, *sustainable and mutually beneficial* approach to international professional volunteering (as the key vector of change).

Arguably, we could have added a new dimension to capture more fully the bi-lateral learning processes and expanded the expectation of system change to cover not only the Ugandan health system but also the NHS.[6] However, at this stage our concern with health systems was primarily with the low-resource setting (Objective 1), the reciprocal component emerging only in individual-level analysis (Objective 2). With these thoughts in mind, the SVP intervention and its evaluation was framed around three potential 'scenarios:'

### Scenario 1: Partial Improvement (Positive Change)

Under this scenario, evidence will indicate that the professional volunteering interventions we are engaging in are at least *partially effective* in promoting systems change. It is important that even this 'partial effect' relates to incremental long-term progress and is not short-lived. Moyo suggests that project evaluations often identify the 'erroneous' impression of AID's success in the shorter term – whilst failing to assess long-term sustainability' (2009: 45).

Policy Implications: Any positive collateral benefits to individual service recipients (Ugandan patients), UK volunteers/health systems are to be identified and encouraged.

### Scenario 2: Neutral Impact (No Change)

Under this scenario, evidence will indicate that the professional volunteering interventions we are engaging are generally *neutral* in terms of systems impact. They neither facilitate nor undermine systems change.

Policy Implications: Positive outcomes for individual service recipients (patients), volunteers (and the UK), free of unintended consequences, may be identified and supported.

## Scenario 3: Negative Impact (Collateral Damage)

Under this scenario, evidence will indicate that the professional volunteering interventions we are engaging are generally *counter-productive/* damaging in terms of promoting long-term (sustainable) improvements in public health systems.

Policy Implications: Any positive gains to individuals (including Ugandan patients) or systems in the UK are tainted with unintended consequences and, on that basis, are unethical and should not be supported.

In this framework, volunteer deployment can be justified provided it meets either Scenario 1 or 2. In Scenario 3 volunteer learning as a goal in its own right cannot be justified and it would be unethical to deploy NHS volunteers to low resource settings in that kind of environment.[7]

This generates important challenges for international placements in the NHS and these have cost implications. First and foremost, to even begin to achieve the outcomes above, volunteer deployment must take place in organisational settings grounded in strong and meaningful relationships and a deep understanding of and commitment to local context. This implies some form of intervention focused on the needs of the host setting. It is not ethical or effective to randomly deploy UK health workers to facilities in low-resource settings as has been the case in the past with medical electives and many missionary style outfits. Investment in the host setting need not and arguably should not imply major financial donations; indeed, we have argued in our sister volume that these are in most cases damaging and counter-productive (Ackers et al. 2016). The major contribution the UK is providing is skilled and willing personnel although carefully planned 'in-kind' contributions may optimise volunteer safety, volunteer learning and host benefits.[8] But it does imply investment in a global health infrastructure and intelligence.

A serious consideration for the NHS and deployment agencies are the operational costs associated with effective volunteer management. These will include a lean but efficient organisational set up in the UK working in close relationship with a lean and efficient receiving organisational team in the host location. In addition to building and investing in relationships with key stakeholder communities in both locations, the team will have an active presence and understand the ever-changing dynamics of context. At present organisations such as THET have relied heavily upon a volunteering ethic to support this infrastructure and many, if not most, health partnerships are managed on a pro bono basis. Unfortunately, this cannot ensure that the most effective and sustained skill base is in place to manage potentially growing volumes of quality-assured international placements.

## Volunteer Management[9]

Once this environment and the relationships that connect it are developed to an adequate level, perhaps through short stay exchanges, volunteer selection processes can be developed in compliance with best practice in UK employment policy. 'Volunteers' by definition are not employees but this should not be seen as a rationale for avoiding or evading sound employment principles. The SVP Model invested considerable effort in advertising/dissemination to raise awareness of opportunities throughout the target community paying particular attention to non-medical cadres who are often neglected in these processes. We then generated a comprehensive recruitment system.

## Transparent and Equitable Recruitment Process

At present, the supply of placements is managed by a disparate range of largely unregulated providers motivated by quite diverse goals. Some of the larger organisations, such as VSO, may be committed to providing equality of opportunity to prospective volunteers. Others may have no interest or experience in this aspect of their work or may utilise quite discriminatory selection criteria. At present, providers operate their own selection systems. A number of SVP volunteers spoke of being rejected by VSO, for example, on the grounds that they were not legally married or, in one case, was a single parent. In another situation, a hosting organisation explicitly discriminated against any volunteers who were not practicing Christians (and requested the insertion of a question in the SVP application form asking for details of the church they currently worshipped at). They also refused to accept volunteers who were not legally married in a heterosexual relationship and made it clear that volunteers were required to attend chapel daily during their placement. These organisations filtering applicants with overt religious 'rules' that fail to comply with UK equality law and policy should not be allowed to provide placements that are affiliated to UK public or charitable organisations.

## AGE AND SENIORITY

Another area of potential tension between the needs of individual volunteers, employing organisations such as the NHS and deploying/hosting organisations concerns age and seniority. Whilst the latter may explicitly prefer more senior or experienced individuals (as noted above) or more mature people perhaps around retirement age who can stay much longer and have fewer pressing family or financial commitments, there is relatively little 'knowledge premium' for the NHS to be made from sending very senior (and expensive) staff towards the end of their career. Interviews with the Army Reservists who play an important, if specific, role in volunteer deployment indicated a strong preference for mid-career individuals who are already highly skilled in their chosen field; primarily clinicians in the 40–45 age group. The interviews suggest that this strategy may prove quite fruitful in identifying and investing in future leaders.

Overall our research would suggest that international exposure at early career level has the sharpest impact on learning; also that early career exposures tend to stimulate ongoing engagement in global health. From an equality perspective sending organisations should see this in the round, balancing the net gains from facilitating early career mobility with the motivational and project-related benefits of mid- and later career engagement. Experienced volunteers with extensive clinical and life experience, particularly if they have worked in low-resource settings offer considerable stability and resilience to composite international teams.

## VOLUNTEER 'MATCHING'

Once a candidate satisfies the deployment criteria, a 'volunteer matching process' ensues in full consultation and with deference to the Health Partnerships engaged on the ground. Unlike organisations such as VSO, the SVP does not advertise detailed positions/roles. Once potential volunteers come forward, it seeks to identify where and how they could contribute to project objectives (including their own learning objectives). Whilst the placement of professional volunteers cannot be supply lead (and focused solely on the needs of prospective volunteers), neither should it be solely demand lead. The articulation of demands from low-resource settings typically places an emphasis on long stays of the most highly qualified staff often with the intention of substituting for local staff. Our research would suggest that this is rarely the most effective form of deployment in capacity-building projects such as the SVP,[10] in terms of the needs of either their volunteers or their employers (the NHS); it does not deliver optimal benefit to the low-resource setting and can be positively detrimental. This is a negotiation process that demands a high level of contextual knowledge of volunteer supply, intervention dynamics and resilient trust relationships. Strachan points to the critical role of relationship building and trust to effective volunteer deployment (2009: 3).

Having identified a potential 'match' the SVP then provides details of the volunteer to the hosting organisation/s. In the SVP case, these organisations are individual health partnerships linking hospitals/universities in the UK with hospitals/universities in Uganda. Wherever possible we link only with public health facilities and strongly advocate that approach in order to support system strengthening rather than the development of parallel systems. One of the unique qualities of the SVP was its basis in a consortium of Health Partnerships known as the Ugandan Maternal and Newborn Hub (the HUB). The HUB was a response to the perceived need for very grounded cooperation and mutual support within the Ugandan HP community; working together in this way enabled us to develop an efficient secretariat that assumed many of the core roles of volunteer management in a democratic environment and wherever possible and appropriate respecting the subsidiarity principle (that individual HPs were primarily responsible for managing their own interventions on the ground).[11] Having this infrastructure and bi-annual volunteer workshops aimed at building relationships and supporting team working gave us the opportunity to support short and longer stay volunteer mobility within Uganda (volunteers could be based across two sites, for example, or teams could get together at certain times for multi-professional interventions).

In theory, other organisations could become involved in this process without undermining the emphasis on deeply contextualised relationships. Health partnerships could act as effective intermediaries linked to commissioning organisations, for example, which is in effect how THET have managed their 'long-term volunteering programme.'[12] Strachan et al. point to the fact that most placements are organised in response to a demand from a deploying or host organisation and most 'sending' organisations do not run placements themselves but use intermediaries for this process (2009: 6/9). However, the more intermediaries become involved the more complex the relationships will be and the greater the potential for poor-quality communication.

The next stage in the SVP process is to set out an initial volunteer role description which then forms the basis of a signed volunteer agreement. The volunteer role description involves direct negotiation between the SVP management team, HP leads and the volunteer in question and seeks to balance the needs of the intervention/s they were contributing to; their own defined learning/career/personal needs, the overall objectives of the SVP and any concerns about risk. The volunteer agreement is in all cases an iterative document[13], and we explain to volunteers that this will go through a process of constant evolution in response to the changing environment and project objectives as well as their own learning and ambitions. In addition to regular email and face-to-face and telephone communication, a monthly reporting mechanism is used to assess progress and identify any concerns/opportunities.

## SUPERVISION, RISK AND THE CO-PRESENCE PRINCIPLE

The principle of 'co-presence' lies at the heart of the SVP volunteer agreement setting out the expectation that every professional volunteer will be working alongside a Ugandan counterpart.[14] As noted in Chapter 4, co-presence is the single most important principle under-pinning a risk mitigated and ethical placement. Mechanisms must be in place to enforce and monitor adherence to co-presence and respond accordingly to breaches of this principle. Individual volunteers and host locations are required to sign up to this commitment. In practice, the long history of breach of conditionality principles in Aid (Moyo 2009) has encouraged a tendency to ignore such principles without reprisal. As such, co-presence takes a long time to embed within a programme and every new volunteer will be faced with the expectation that they will go on rotas and engage directly in service delivery. As noted above many professional volunteers, especially doctors, will be tempted to ignore the commitment to co-presence, especially if they interpret this as a challenge to their primary commitment to individual patient care (for a discussion see Ackers et al. 2016). This underlines the need to impress on every volunteer that they are one member of a complex intervention and must comply with project objectives and principles; managing volunteers in this way demands an investment in infrastructure both in the UK and on the ground. Volunteer induction is a critical component of the 'volunteer journey'.

## BUILDING RELATIONSHIPS WITH PROFESSIONAL VOLUNTEERS: INDUCTION THROUGH TO DEBRIEFING

Much of the international placement literature argues that adequate support before, during and after international placements optimises learning and impact. Certainly volunteer induction is critical to effective deployment (Gedde et al. 2011). Induction is commonly associated with a physical 'induction pack'. In the SVP we assessed existing products and on the basis of our risk assessment developed a 'pack' tailored to the local context. In practice this is a living document continually adapted over time as new challenges or opportunities/resources emerge. Some discussion has taken place over the relative merits of formal induction meetings either in the UK or in the host setting. However, the original plan of holding group meetings either in-country or in the UK has been amended to provide more individual-based approaches largely not only because volunteers are coming and going at all times of year (and not in blocks as originally anticipated) but also because many were unable to commit to week long programmes prior to departure. In practice, the SVP has combined interviews and face-to-face meetings with measures to connect new volunteers to the wider volunteer and project community.

As important as preparation, the literature on placement learning not only emphasises the importance of reflection both in terms of translating and applying knowledge but also mitigating trauma or culture shock on return (Briscoe 2013; Clampin 2008). According to Kolb (1983), reflection is a key component of experiential learning and much of this reflection continues to happen post return (Murdoch-Eaton 2014). Protagonists of 'transformational learning theory' emphasise the longitudinal quality of volunteer learning as individuals consolidate their new knowledge into existing schemas (Fee and Gray 2013). In the SVP model, we have tended not to view this as before-and-after events but rather as a continuous relationship-building process linking volunteers not only into project management teams but also and perhaps most importantly with previous, existing and future volunteers to build volunteer communities. From a volunteer deployment perspective, our strong preference now is to locate volunteers in clusters encouraging cross-professional and inter-generational mentoring and support. We have found that both optimise impacts in host settings and opportunities for volunteer learning, creating active co-supervision and co-learning contexts. Importantly this is also a cornerstone of risk mitigation.

These processes are labour intensive and rest on the quality of personal relationships and active knowledge of project interventions on the ground. Whilst larger organisations may have the volume of volunteers to support and require intense pre-placement induction and de-briefing, we would argue that it is detailed knowledge of activity on the ground that is most important in supporting volunteer deployment.

Responsibility for volunteer induction in the SVP context was shared throughout the management team with HP leads contributing to the induction pack and playing a critical role in in-country volunteer induction. Wherever possible new volunteers accompany or join one of the HP leads. We also encourage volunteers to 'overlap' so that they can support each other and encourage continuity in project interventions (whilst being cautious about labour substitution[15]).

## RISK MITIGATION AND ADMINISTRATIVE ISSUES

Once a volunteer placement has been planned and the volunteer agreement set out our in-country support manager sets processes in motion to ensure that every volunteer has the necessary clinical registration and visa/work permits. We have referred (above) to the importance of conditionality and reciprocity. In practice, receiving countries are accustomed to behave as the passive 'recipients' of Aid with little interest in or attention to the risks involved. The Ugandan Maternal and New-born HUB with the assistance of the UK-Uganda Health Workforce Alliance[16] has established a smoother system so that volunteers now obtain their clinical registration prior to arrival and work permits within the first three months of their stay (when entry visas expire). Following ongoing lobbying by the SVP we have managed to secure work permits at no cost; we are currently pushing to reduce the costs associated with clinical registration.

The SVP purchased a bespoke health insurance plan suitable for volunteers engaged in hands-on clinical work; most existing off the peg insurance policies are not suitable for professional volunteers. As managers we felt it was important to have all the volunteers covered by one policy so that all volunteers are aware of procedures and emergency contact details (included in the induction pack). This process is relatively expensive.

Despite considerable effort and lobbying over the last five years, it has become even more difficult to provide professional indemnity insurance cover for professional volunteers. For the first three years of the SVP, doctors could receive cover from the Medical Protection Society (MPS) or the Medical Defence Union (MDU). Since then, both organisations have tightened up and are giving it only on a case-by-case basis. In the case of the MDU they require details that adequate supervision is in place. The Royal College of Nursing (RCN) covers all its members including students and this extends to midwives registered with the RCN. However, the Royal College of Midwives refuses to extend professional indemnity cover to any of its members leaving a significant loophole in cover. More detail on risk management including protocols on HIV prophylaxis and Ebola are contained in the SVP Volunteer induction pack on the Knowledge for Change Charity website (www.knowledgeforchange.org.uk/).

## NOTES

1. This has been explicitly recognised in the MOVE project through the assessment of the potential for a psychometric tool to assess the learning outcomes deriving from international placements.
2. From 2017/18, new students on nursing, midwifery and allied health professional pre-registration courses (which lead on to qualification with one of the health professional regulators) in England will take out maintenance and tuition loans like other students rather than getting an NHS grant (Council of Deans of Health 2016)
3. VSO are currently reviewing this policy and encouraging shorter stays.
4. Valuable learning also takes place at this level and many of the actors will be senior UK clinicians (and evaluators) but the primary objective of these visits will be to enable the learning of others.
5. www.mercyships.org.uk/
6. We paid some lip service to the NHS as a system in the scenarios but this was not a focus of our intervention at that point in time. Our current work involving undergraduates is more explicitly holistic.
7. We assume that similar assumptions will be made by NHS facilities hosting undergraduate students.
8. A simple example here would be the work SVP volunteers undertook in a multidisciplinary team to effect the opening of a large facility which then became a valuable placement site (Ackers 2014).
9. Strachan (2009) and Comhlamh (2016) provide excellent guidelines on ethical volunteering.
10. We would expect this to be different in emergency relief organisations.
11. An area of considerable tension concerned delegation of principles of equality and fair deployment which were challenged repeatedly by the UK lead of a mission hospital.
12. http://www.thet.org/our-work/what-we-do

13. Strachan et al. emphasise the importance of volunteer 'flexibility' ad a willingness to respond to changing demands and circumstances (2009: 10).
14. This is discussed in Chapter 4 and in footnote 6.
15. In some cases we deliberately planned gaps in volunteer deployment to assess where interventions had led to behaviour change on the ground and reduce the risks associated with dependency. Continuity of project does not necessarily imply continuous presence in a particular health facility.
16. The 'Alliance' was established in 2013 By Lord Crisps following a high-level meeting with the Ugandan Ministry of health. In practice its activity has been quite minimal until it was recently received support from THET and the Global Health Exchange (GHE): http://www.globalhealthexchange. co.uk/projects/uukha/

# Appendix 1

# Data Collection and Methods

This was a qualitative, interview-based study which broadly utilised the principles of grounded theory (Glaser and Strauss 1967). Therefore, rather than basing out explorations on a firm hypothesis, we attempted to develop a plausible representation of the worldview in which our participants were embedded and engaged in a research strategy which incorporated the ongoing analysis, comparison and theorising. The purpose of utilising semi-structured interviews was to achieve an understanding of varying conceptualisations of professional volunteering, the different meanings it had for people and its place in their lives and career planning. We also wanted to explore more mundane issues such as how professional placements worked for people on a practical level; how and why they undertook them; what people thought they got out of them; and how these experiences impacted their work and career once they returned to the NHS.

## Interviews

Our primary corpus of in-depth semi-structured interviews comprised a wide range of returned volunteers and other stakeholders ($n$ = 51). These data were collected during 2014 and 2015 and included a representative sample of NHS employees which was designed to broadly reflect the current spread of staff across all grades.[1] The sample comprised 11 qualified or trainee doctors 16 nurses and midwives; 6 clinical support staff; 10

© The Author(s) 2017                                                    109
H.L. Ackers et al., *Healthcare, Frugal Innovation, and Professional Voluntarism*, DOI 10.1007/978-3-319-48366-5

managerial and administrative staff; and 8 'others', which included ambulance and maintenance staff, cleaners and caterers etc. Of the entire sample, 8 respondents (15%) had not been on a placement or had no overseas experience. We initially recruited participants via our existing NHS contacts based at the University of Salford, and the University of Manchester Medical School. A significant proportion of volunteer or ex-volunteer respondents were contacted via established links with organisations that provided overseas placements.

We were fortunate in that half of the research team had extensive experience working in the field of overseas development and professional placement provision, and the other half in NHS training evaluation and healthcare research. This gave us a broad base of primary contacts connected and whom we were able to access. We placed only broad restrictions on which individuals we approached, and recruitment of participants was routinely snowballed from an initial contact with a key player, for example, a returned professional volunteer or a charity administrator volunteer. This person provided an all-important level of legitimisation to other potential interviewees. Connections and subsequent interview opportunities tended to develop organically from here. This approach was informed by an understanding of professional volunteering charities and how they are embedded in a web of other groups and networks that intersect with the NHS. Interview recruitment was continued until saturation was achieved. That is, until the process was adding nothing new to our understanding of a given theme.

We used qualitative and semi-structured interviews, and these were always conducted informally. This enabled us to adapt to the variety of positions and perspectives that were in evidence. Our interview schedules (i.e. the questions we asked and the themes we chose to explore) were continually reviewed and revised as necessary on the basis of emerging evidence, and we individually tailored the interviews of each interviewee. We explicitly pursued negative cases as a means of enhancing the validity of our propositions as they developed. In the context of this study, this particularly meant talking to staff and stakeholders who were not actively engaged in professional volunteering, as well as those who were, to those who had experienced barriers to involvement and so forth. There were, however, a number of thematic elements which were addressed in every case. These were as follows: (1) their basic demographic information; (2) their relationship to, or role within the NHS (doctor, nurse, placement provider etc.); (3) their experiences of being on a professional placement abroad; (4) the way these experiences had affected or changed them; (5) the processes they had gone through to get a placement; (6) barriers or enabling influences they had encountered and barriers they could see being an issue for other people; (7) finally – particularly in the case of returned volunteers who were back in their NHS roles – we wanted to explore the impact of their experience on their everyday work, and on their relationships with the colleagues and patients, now that they were back in the UK.

These themes formed the basis for the majority of interviews, although again the specifics of individual cases and their particular relation to a given group often meant that the interview format we actually used differed quite widely between participants. Interviews were audio-recorded where possible and transcribed verbatim. Analysis of transcription data was conducted alongside ongoing analysis of data from our other main sources.

## DOCUMENTARY ANALYSIS

During the course of the MOVE project, we collected a very wide range of documents and other media. This material helped us contextualise the findings that we generated from our other sources, but also often provided useful tangential trigger points for our analysis. We looked at publicity material and formal documentation from a range of relevant organisation; official and unofficial policy documentation; information and marketing material from placement providers; internal auditing and evaluation material (SVP project); NHS and DOH statistical data; personal diaries and blogs written by participants; and photo, video and audio material. Our selection of material was informed both by our initial research questions and by themes that were emerging during the course of the study. The importance of documents and media varied. However, we were deliberately eclectic in our definition of what we considered to be relevant, and as a result, only a proportion of the large corpus we amassed were actually incorporated into our analysis.

## ETHNOGRAPHIC AND OBSERVATIONAL WORK

Ethnography was not initially intended to be one of our primary methods. However, in the course of the study, the research team, many of whom had other roles organising volunteer work (see Ackers and Johnson 2016) had the opportunity to undertake several field trips to sub-Saharan Africa.

There, they were able to conduct participant and non-participant observation with long-term professional volunteers in the field. We were also able to undertake background ethnographic observation while accompanying groups of student doctors and nurses on shorter-term elective placement trips to Uganda and Central Southern India during 2015–2016. Subsequently, this observational material made a very useful addition to our primary corpus and our appreciation of the context in which professional volunteers – in a developing country at least – are required to work.

The actual observational work carried out was therefore quite varied and opportunistic. It ranged from spending time with professional volunteers in the field, primarily doctors, anaesthetists, nurses and midwives, but also biomedical engineers and administrators. We were able to observe them as they worked and saw how the environments they engaged with influenced what they did. We were also able to obtain data from 'around' these environments to enable everyday detail of the setting to emerge. These included 'satellite' encounters, such as those which might occur between UK volunteers and local staff or between local staff and patients when UK staff were not present. Observations like this helped clarify and flesh out some of the more subtle cultural interrelations that were reported and allowed us to compare the reported perspectives of volunteers (as relayed in interviews etc.), with direct observations of ongoing behavioural dynamics.

## DATA FROM THE SUSTAINABLE VOLUNTEERING PROJECT (SVP)

We were fortunate to have full access to a large corpus of the interview and ethnographic data collected as part of the *Sustainable Volunteering Project.* This was a separate action-based research study that pre-dated MOVE, and which provided us with some significant data – particularly relating to narrative accounts and interviews with current and returning (NHS) professional volunteers engaged in work in sub-Saharan Africa. A full outline of the *Sustainable Volunteering Project* (SVP) is given in Appendix 2, but broadly, the data we were able to access were originally collected as part of an extensive internal evaluation programme which was carried out for the duration of the project. These data included the following:

1. Pre-, mid-, and post-placement interviews with long-term volunteers
2. Monthly reports (containing qualitative and quantitative data)

3. Interviews with the Ugandan Health Facility management and staff
4. Interviews with UMNH partnership coordinators
5. Interviews with mentors
6. Recorded workshops and focus groups
7. Site visits and observations made by the LMP evaluation team

We were also able to gain access to a large collection of email correspondence between volunteers in the field and SVP staff. This corpus is particularly interesting, as it is composed mainly of material relating to long-term volunteers. Most of the SVP volunteers, for example, were in a country for at least three months, and personnel frequently stay for over a year. This length of stay is relatively uncommon for NHS-based professional volunteers taking time out for work-related or ongoing training placements (the average stay being around a month), but could be argued to be most impactful – in the context of both the volunteers themselves and the country they are working in. In the context of this book, we are not specifically concerned with arguments over the benefits or otherwise that professional volunteering has on local populations, but with these types of extended stay, a whole raft of subtle, in-depth, contextual knowledge becomes available to an in-country person who would not necessarily be apparent to those engaged for shorter periods.

## ETHICAL APPROVAL

Ethical approval for the MOVE study was obtained from the University of Manchester Research Ethics Committee and the University of Salford Research Ethics Committee in 2014. As an independent evaluation-based enterprise, the SVP project was not subject to formal academic or NHS ethical approval. Permission to use these data on a case-by-case basis was obtained from the Tropical Health Education Trust (which funded the SVP) and the appropriate project steering groups.

## NOTE

1. In recruiting to the study, we aimed to broadly match the proportions of respondents from each staff cadre with current actual staffing levels within the NHS.

# Appendix 2

# The Sustainable Volunteering Project

## Background and Objectives

The Sustainable Volunteering Project (SVP) is managed by the Liverpool-Mulago Partnership (LMP) and was initially funded by the UK Department for International Development via the Tropical Health Education Trust's Health Partnership Scheme. Financial support has also been received from the Royal College of Obstetricians and Gynaecologists (RCOG) and the Association of Anaesthetists of Great Britain and Ireland (AAGBI). The THET-funded project began in April 2012 and ran for a three-year period, ending March 2015. The SVP continues and is now funded in association with our partner charity Knowledge for Change (www.knowlege4change.org.uk/)

The LMP had been placing professional volunteers in Kampala for over four years before applying for funding for the SVP. The SVP, however, marked a substantial increase in the scale and scope of this activity, widening the LMP's focus outside of Kampala to support other Health Partnerships involved within the Ugandan Maternal & Newborn Hub (UMNH) and also broadening the cadres of Health Professionals supported to include not only obstetricians but also paediatricians, anaesthetists, midwives, nurses and biomedical engineers.

UMNH is a consortium of UK-Uganda Health Partnerships established by the LMP in 2011 and encompassing the LMP, the Basingstoke-Hoima Partnership for Health, the Gulu-Manchester Health Partnership, the PONT-Mbale Partnership, the Bristol-Mbarara

© The Author(s) 2017
H.L. Ackers et al., *Healthcare, Frugal Innovation, and Professional Voluntarism*, DOI 10.1007/978-3-319-48366-5

Link, the Kisiizi-Chester Partnership, the Kisiizi-Reading Partnership and a partnership between Salford University, Mountains of the Moon University and the Kabarole Health District.

The professional volunteers complete placements of varying lengths (between 6 and 24 months) and engage in a variety of initiatives, training programmes and on-the-job mentoring schemes which aim to increase capacity and improve the skills of the health workers, both in Uganda and in the UK. The SVP's focus is on capacity building, and systems change and its objectives are twofold:

1. To support evidence-based, holistic and sustainable systems change through improved knowledge transfer, translation and impact
2. To promote a more effective, sustainable and mutually beneficial approach to international professional volunteering (as the key vector of change)

The SVP does not have a focus on service delivery or workforce substitution as this activity is not judged to be sustainable.

## VOLUNTEER MANAGEMENT AND SUPPORT

All SVP volunteers are recruited, selected and managed by the LMP (and more recently also K4C). The main organisations targeted during the initial LTV recruitment were the Royal Colleges of Obstetrics and Gynaecology, Anaesthetists, Nursing and Midwives. The Royal Colleges either circulated an advertisement by email or posted it on their websites. The advertisements were also circulated by UMNH members to their local deaneries and hospitals. This initial advertisement process was successful in raising sufficient interest from prospective LTVs, the key to the success being the LMP's ability to utilise the existing links and networks established over previous years. As the project matured, an increasing number of LTVs were recruited through word-of-mouth advertisement by previous SVP LTV's and during project dissemination events, national and international conferences and workshops. Examples of such events include the British Maternal and Foetal Medicine Society's 'Annual Conference' (2013), the AAGBI's 'World Anaesthesia Society Conference' (2013), the Global Women's Research Society Conference (2012) and the Development Studies Association's 'Annual Conference' (2013).

## SELECTION

Following an initial expression of interest, two processes are run simultaneously before a candidate can be recruited to the SVP. The first process
involves prospective LTVs completing an application form and attending an
interview (usually face-to-face) in order to ascertain, for example, whether a
candidate would be suitable, when and why they wish to undertake a
placement, what support they might require, what they hope to achieve
and what skills they possess which would be of benefit to the health system
in Uganda. Two references are required to objectively verify a candidate's
suitability and identify any additional support they may require.

The second process involves circulating the candidates' details to UMNH
partnerships to assess which of them would be interested in hosting the
candidate should they be recruited to the SVP. This process was designed to
align the supply of LTVs with demand on the ground in Uganda and the
ability of the local UMNH partnerships to host them. An LTV is only
recruited if both of the selection processes yielded positive results.

## PLACEMENT LOGISTICS

The subsequent stage following an LTV's recruitment is their pre-placement induction. Each LTV is provided with a comprehensive induction
pack containing useful information on UMNH placement locations, what
to expect in Uganda, placement logistics and travel, insurance and emergency contact details, health and safety and advice on pensions and other
personal finances. LTVs receive a 'volunteer agreement' to sign and return
to LMP management which outlines the LMP's organisational expecta-
tions, a code of conduct, a statement on co-presence, potential disciplinary
procedures and a personalised role description. Volunteer agreements are
drawn up in conjunction with the LTV, the relevant UMNH partner
organisation and the in-country counterparts to maximise stakeholder
involvement and ensure all parties remain informed and satisfied.

Each placement location/facility and all LTV accommodation were
professionally risk assessed at the beginning of the SVP. This risk assessment is shared with LTVs in advance of their placement, advising them of
the potential risks of placements in Uganda, how the risks can be mitigated
and what to do in the case that the risk materialises. The LMP also
purchased a bespoke and comprehensive travel and medical insurance
policy at the beginning of the SVP to cover all LTVs, ensuring each of

them had adequate and sufficient cover throughout their placements. Having one familiar and reliable insurance policy and emergency contact number for all LTVs is beneficial in terms of project management and reduces individual LTVs and organisational risk.

In addition to insurance, the LMP also arranges LTV flights, clinical registration, visa/work permit, accommodation, airport transfers and the majority of placement related travel in line with the recommendations of the risk assessment. The risk and logistical burden put on LTVs is reduced by, for example, using safe and reliable drivers for travel, only selecting flights that arrive at suitable times and only using safe and risk assessed accommodation. Controlling these processes centrally allows for better coordination and achieves some economies of scale in terms of the procurement.

## PLACEMENT SUPPORT

LTVs have access to a wide range of support during their placements. In terms of financial support, LTVs receive a monthly stipend to assist them in covering their costs at home and in Uganda. The stipend is paid directly into their bank account, with the initial payment being made on the date of their outbound flight and consecutive recurrent payments made at monthly intervals. The Tropical Health Education Trust's Health Partnership Scheme is able to fund the employer and employee pension contributions of those LTVs previously employed by the UK NHS for the duration of their placements, marking a less direct yet potentially hugely beneficial provision of financial support for LTVs.

Each LTV is assigned a UK and a Ugandan mentor to provide clinical, mental and pastoral support and advice during their placement. Suitable mentors are selected by the LMP in collaboration with UMNH partners and in-country stakeholders, and usually come from the same disciplinary background as the LTV, as well as having previous experience of working/volunteering in Uganda. Many of the UK mentors selected are themselves former SVP LTVs that have returned to the UK but are keen to retain links with the project. The mentors serve as the first point of contact for LTVs; however, frequent communication with LMP management is also encouraged in case any problems arise that the mentors cannot deal with. LTVs provide written reports to LMP management on a monthly basis so their health and well-being can be monitored.

SVP workshops are held every six months. All SVP LTVs and stakeholders are invited to attend along with other LTVs working on similar projects, for example, the 'Global Links' project run by the Royal College of Paediatrics and Children's Health. Each LTV conducts a short presentation detailing their placement activity, successes and any challenges faced. The events stimulate useful discussion and learning and enable the LTVs to build networks which provide platforms for effective peer-to-peer support, partnership and co-working.

## PROJECT EVALUATION

An extensive and comprehensive evaluation programme has been carried out for the duration of the SVP. Data is collected by LMP management and evaluation teams, PhD students and the LTVs themselves for evaluation purposes and includes the following:

1. Pre-, mid- and post-placement interviews with LTVs
2. LTV written monthly reports (containing qualitative and quantitative data)
3. Interviews with Ugandan Health Facility management and staff
4. Interviews with UMNH partnership coordinators
5. Interviews with LTV mentors
6. Recorded workshops and focus groups
7. Site visits and observations made by the LMP evaluation team
8. Logging of stakeholder email communication
9. Reviews of new and existing literature relating to professional volunteering
10. Publications and presentations conducted by the LTVs at conferences and other dissemination events

All data is collected, anonymised, coded and analysed using Nvivo software. The SVP has evolved and strengthened on an iterative basis since its beginning in April 2012, based on the outcomes of the project evaluation and the growing experience of the project managers.

### Volunteer Deployment in the SVP

The SVP placed 44 professional volunteers across the UMNH partnership locations over the course of the initial three-year period between April 2012 and March 2015, achieving a combined total of 358 'volunteer months'. The total number of volunteer months spent at each UMNH location is illustrated below in Fig. A.1. The average (mean) placement

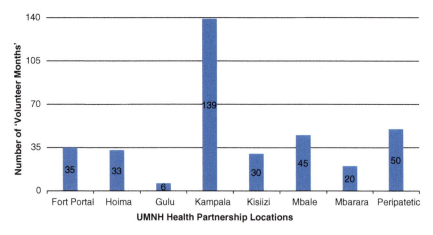

**Fig. A.1**  Number of 'volunteer months' spent at each UMNH health partnership location

duration across all disciplines was 8.1 months; however, the most common placement duration (modal average) was six months. The shortest placement duration was one month (the volunteer ended their six months placement early) and the longest placement was 26 months.

The professional volunteers came from nine broad professional backgrounds; the highest number coming from Anaesthesiology (10) and

**Table A.1**  SVP volunteers by professional background

| Health professional disciplinary background | Number deployed during the SVP | Total combined number of volunteer months |
|---|---|---|
| Anaesthetists | 10 | 71 |
| Obstetricians | 9 | 60 |
| Midwives | 8 | 60 |
| Nurses | 6 | 48 |
| Foundation year 2 doctors | 4 | 30 |
| Paediatricians | 3 | 33 |
| Social scientists | 2 | 24 |
| Biomedical engineers | 1 | 26 |
| General practitioners | 1 | 6 |
| Total: | 44 | 358 |

*Source*: Created by the authors.

the lowest number coming from General Practice (1) and Biomedical Engineering (1). Table A.1 details the number of volunteers deployed from each of the disciplinary backgrounds and the total number of volunteer placement months completed. Multidisciplinary team working was a key feature within the SVP and was believed to be the most effective way of achieving the desired outcomes of the project.

# APPENDIX 3

# THE MOVE SURVEY

© The Author(s) 2017
H.L. Ackers et al., *Healthcare, Frugal Innovation, and Professional Voluntarism*, DOI 10.1007/978-3-319-48366-5

## Measuring the Outcomes of Volunteering for Education

1)    Staff Group

☐ Allied health professionals
☐ Healthcare scientists
☐ Medical and dental
☐ NHS Infrastructure
☐ Scientific and technical
☐ Qualified Ambulance staff
☐ Nursing, midwifery and health vis
☐ Support to clinical staff

2)    Career stage

Pre-University
Student
Early career
Mid career
Experienced
Post retirement

3)    Age

☐ Below 25
☐ 26-30
☐ 31-40
☐ 42-50
☐ 51-60
☐ 61-70
☐ 71 or over

4)    Gender

☐ Male
☐ Female
☐ Other

5)    Nationality

☐ British
☐ European
☐ Non-EU National – High income Country
☐ Non-EU National – Low income Country
☐ Other

6) Have you had **any periods in another country, either as an employee or volunteer?**

☐ Yes
☐ No

**Placement 1   (form included space for multiple placements)**

What kind of placement was it?

☐ Healthcare
☐ Other

Economic status of country:

☐ High income
☐ Mid income
☐ Low income

What stage of your career were you at?

☐ Pre-degree
☐ Degree / training
☐ Early career
☐ Mid career
☐ Senior
☐ Retirement

7)    Would you be happy to be interviewed about your experience as a volunteer abroad?

Name

Email / phone number

**Fig. A.2**   Measuring the outcomes of volunteering for education

# REFERENCES

Ackers, H. L. (2003). *The participation of women researchers in the TMR Marie Curie Fellowships.* Brussels: European Commission.

Ackers, H. L. (2008). Internationalisation, mobility and metrics: A new form of indirect discrimination? *Minerva, 46*(4), 410–435.

Ackers, H. L. (2010). Internationalisation and equality: The contribution of short stay mobility to progression in science careers. *Journal Recherches Sociologiques Et Anthropologiques, XLI*(1), 83–103.

Ackers, H. L. (2014). Improving referral systems to reduce congestion and maternal delays in Uganda. SVP Policy Report. SVP. www.knowledge4 change.org. Accessed 19 October 2016.

Ackers, H. L. (2015). Mobilities and knowledge transfer: Understanding the contribution of volunteer stays to North-South healthcare partnerships'. *International Migration, 53*(1), 131–147.

Ackers, H. L., & Ackers-Johnson, J. (2014). *Understanding 'co-presence' in the sustainable volunteering project.* Unpublished internal report, Sustainable Volunteering Project.

Ackers, H. L., & Gill, B. (2007). *Moving people and knowledge: Scientific mobility in an Enlarged European Union.* London: Edward Elgar.

Ackers, H. L., & Gill, B. (2008). *Doctoral mobility in the social sciences,* NORFACE ERA-NET. http://www.norface.net/wp-content/uploads/2015/09/Doctoral_Mobility.pdf. Accessed 19 October 2016.

Ackers, H. L., Ioannou, E., & Ackers-Johnson, J. (2016). The impact of delays on maternal and neonatal outcomes in Ugandan public health facilities: The role of absenteeism. *Health Policy and Planning,* 1–10. doi: 10.1093/heapol/czw046.

© The Author(s) 2017
H.L. Ackers et al., *Healthcare, Frugal Innovation, and Professional Voluntarism,* DOI 10.1007/978-3-319-48366-5

Addicott, R., Maguire, D., Honeyman, M., & Jabbal, J. (2015). *Workforce planning in the NHS*. London: The Kings Fund.

Ahmed, A., Ackers-Johnson, J., & Ackers, H. L. (2017). *The ethics of healthcare education placements in low-income countries: First do no harm?*. London: Palgrave.

All-Party Parliamentary Group on Global Health. (2013). *Improving health at home and abroad: How overseas volunteering from the NHS benefits the UK and the world*. London: House of Commons.

Appleby, J., Thompson, J., & Jabbal, J. (2016). How is the NHS performing. *Quarterly Monitoring Report 19*.

Arthur, M. B. (1994). The boundaryless career: A new perspective for organizational inquiry. *Journal of Organizational Behaviour, 15*, 295–306.

Arthur, M. B., & Rousseau, D. M. (1996). *The boundaryless career: A new employment principle for a new organizational era*. Oxford: Oxford University Press.

Baguley, D., Killeen, T., & Wright, J. (2006). International health links: An evaluation of partnerships between healthcare organizations in the UK and developing countries. *Tropical Doctor, 36*(3), 149–154.

Banatvala, N., & Macklow-Smith, A. (1997). Integrating overseas work with an NHS career. *BMJ, 314*(7093), 2–2. doi: 10.1136/bmj.314.7093.2.

Barclay, S., Todd, C., Finlay, I., Grande, G., & Wyatt, P. (2002). Not another questionnaire! Maximizing the response rate, predicting non-response and assessing non-response bias in postal questionnaire studies of GPs. *Family Practice, 19*(1), 105–111.

Baruch, Y., & Hall, D. T. (2004). The academic career: A new perspective for organisational enquiry. *Journal of Organisational Behaviour, 15*, 295–306.

Baruch, Y., & Holtom, B. C. (2008). Survey response rate levels and trends in organizational research. *Human Relations, 61*(8), 1139–1160.

Baruch, Y., & Reis, C. (2015). Boundaryless careers and how boundaryless are also global careers?. *Challenges and a Theoretical Perspective, Thunderbird International Business Review*, Feature Article.

Bernard, K., Graitcer, P., & Vlugt, T. E. A. (1989). Epidemiological surveillance in peace coprs volunteers: A model for monitoring heath in temporary residents of developing countries. *International Journal of Epidemiology, 1*(18), 220–225.

Bhatta, P., Simkhada, P., Van Teijlingen, E., & Maybin, S. (2009). A questionnaire study of voluntary service overseas (VSO) volunteers: Health, risk and problems encountered. *Journal of Travel Medicine, 16*, 332–337.

Boffey, D. (2014, 23rd November). Number of GPs seeking to leave UK and work abroad doubles under coalition. *The Guardian.*.

Boyd, M. (1989). Family and personal networks in international migration: Recent developments and new agendas. *International Migration Review, 23*(3), 638–670.

Bresnen, M., Hodgson, D., Bailey, S. et al. (2014). Being a manager, becoming a professional? A case study and interview-based exploration of the use of management knowledge across communities of practice in health-care organisations. *Health Services and Delivery Research, 214*.

Briscoe, L. (2013). Becoming culturally sensitive: A painful process?. *Midwifery*, *29*(6), 559–565.

British Medical Association. (2009). *Broadening your horizons: A guide to taking time out to work and train in developing countries*. BMA.

Buchan, J. (2001). Nurse Migration and international recruitment. *Nursing Inquiry*, *8*(4), 203–204.

Bussell, H., & Forbes, D. (2002). Understanding the volunteer market: The what, where, who and why of volunteering. *International Journal of Nonprofit and Voluntary Sector Marketing*, *7*(3), 244–257. doi: 10.1002/nvsm.183.

Button, L., Green, B., Tengnah, C., Johansson, I., & Baker, C. (2005). The impact of international placements on nurses' personal and professional lives: Literature review. *Journal of Advanced Nursing*, *50*(3), 315–324. doi: 10.1111/j.1365-2648.2005.03395.x.

Chartered Institute of Personnel and Development (2014). *Volunteering to learn: Employee development through community action*. London.

Clampin, A. (2008). Overseas placements: Addressing our challenges? *The British Journal of Occupational Therapy*, *71*(8), 354–356.

Comhlamh. (Irish aid) code of good practice. www.comhlamh.org.

Council of Deans of Health. (2016). The 2015 spending review changes to nursing, Midwifery and AHP education – background information for students. http://www.councilofdeans.org.uk/2015/11/the-2015-spending-review-changes-to-nursing-midwifery-and-ahp-education-background-information-for-students/.

Cox, D. (2008). Evidence of the main factors inhibiting mobility and career development of researchers. *Final Report to the European Commission*. Contract DG-RTD-2005-M-02-01. http://ec.europa.eu/euraxess/pdf/research_policies/rindicate_final_report_2008_11_june_08_v4.pdf. Accessed 19 October 2016.

Crisp, N. (2010). *Turning the world upside down: The search for global health in the 21st century*. London: Royal Society of Medicine Press Ltd.

Crisp, N. (2014). Mutual learning and reverse innovation; where next? *Globalization and Health*, *10*(1), 14. doi: 10.1186/1744-8603-10-14.

Dean, E. (2013). Tanzania changed me. *Nursing Standard (Royal College of Nursing (Greatbritain)*, *27*(52), 16–17.

DeFillippi, R. J., & Arthur, M. B. (1994). The boundaryless career: A competency based perspective. *Journal of Organisational Behaviour*, *15*, 124–139.

Department of Health. (2001). *Working together, learning together: A framework for lifelong learning for the NHS*. London: Department of Health.

Department of Health. (2010A). The framework for NHS involvement in international development. http://www.severndeanery.nhs.uk/assets/Internationalisation/. Accessed 8 March 2016.

Donnelly, L., & Mulhern, M. (2012, 13th May.). NHS pays £20,000 a week for a doctor. *The Telegraph*.

Dowell, J., Blacklock, C., Liao, C., & Merrylees, N. (2014). Boost or burden? Issues posed by short placements in resource-poor settings. *The British Journal of General Practice: The Journal of the Royal College of General Practitioners*, 64(623), 272–273. doi: 10.3399/bjgp14X679945.

Dowell, J., & Merrylees, N. (2009). Electives: Isn't it time for a change? *Medical Education*, 43, 121–126. doi: 10.1111/j.1365-2923.2008.03253.x.

Ericsson, K. A., Krampe, R. T., & Tesch-Romer, C. (1993). The role of deliberate practice in the acquisition of expert performance. *Psychological Review*, 100(3), 363–406.

Evans, J. R., & Mathur, A. (2005). The value of online surveys. *Internet Research*, 15(2), 195–219.

Fee, A., & Gray, S. J. (2013). Transformational learning experiences of international development volunteers in the Asia-Pacific: The case of a multinational NGO. *Journal of World Business*, 48(2), 196–208.

Ferro, A. (2006). Desired mobility or satisfied immobility? Migratory aspirations among knowledge workers. *Journal of Education and Work*, 19(2), 171–200.

Francis, R. (2013). *Report of the mid Staffordshire NHS foundation trust public inquiry*. London: HMSO.

Gedde, M., Edjang, S., & Mandeville, K. (2011). *Working in international health*. Oxford: Oxford University Press.

General Medical Council. (2009). *Tomorrow's doctors – outcomes and standards for undergraduate medical education*. London: GMC, 1–108.

Glaser, B., & Strauss, S. (1967). *The discovery of grounded theory: Strategies for qualitative research*. Chicago: Aldine Publishing Company.

Go Overseas. (2014). https://www.gooverseas.com/. accessed 1 November 2016.

Graitcer, B. K. P., Vlugt, T. et al. (1989). Epidemiological surveillance in peace corps volunteers: A model for monitoring health in temporary residents of developing countries. *The International Journal of Epidemiology*, 18, 220–225.

Greatrex-White, S. (2008). Uncovering study abroad: Foreignness and its relevance to nurse education and cultural competence. *Nurse Education Today*, 28(5), 530–538.

Grover, A., Caulfield, P., & Roehrich, K J (2014). *Frugal innovation in healthcare and its applicability to developed markets*. London: University of Bath.

Harland, T. (2003). Vygotsky's zone of proximal development and problem-based learning: Linking a theoretical concept with practice through action research. *Teaching in Higher Education*, 8(2), 263–272. doi: 10.1080/1356251032000052483.

Heath, S. (2007). Widening the gap: Pre-university gap years and the 'economy of experience'. *British Journal of Sociology of Education*, 28(1), 89–103.

Health Education England (2014). The health education England strategic framework. https://www.hee.nhs.uk/our-work/planning-commissioning/strategic-framework. Accessed 01 November 2016.

Health Education England. (2016A). *Medical recruitment.* https://hee.nhs.uk/our-work/attracting-recruiting/medical-recruitment. Accessed 11 October 2016.

Health Education England. (2016B). *Financial planning.* https://www.hee.nhs.uk/our-work/planning-commissioning/financial-planning. Accessed 27 May 2016.

Health Education England. (2016C). https://hee.nhs.uk/. Accessed 01 November 2016.

Hockey, P., Tobin, A., Kemp, J., Kerrigan, J., Kitsell, F., Green, P., Sewell, A., Smith, C., Stanwick, S., & Lees, P. (2009). Global health partnerships: Leadership development for a purpose. *Leadership in Health Services, 22*(4), 306–316.

Horton, A. (2009). Internationalising occupational therapy education. *The British Journal of Occupational Therapy, 72*(5), 227–230. doi: 10.1177/030802260907200511.

Hudson, S., & Inkson, K. (2006). Volunteer overseas development workers: The hero's adventure and personal transformation. *Career Development International, 4,* 304–320.

Hughes, D., & Clarke, V. (2016). Thousands of NHS nursing and doctor posts lie vacant. *BBC News.*

IBM SPSS Statistics for Windows *Version 22.0.* Armonk, NY: IBM Corp.

Iredale, R. (2001). The migration of professionals: Theories and typologies. *International Migration, 39*(5), 7–24.

Jones, A., Knights, D. P., Sinclair, V. F., & Baraitser, P. (2013). Do health partnerships with organisations in lower income countries benefit the UK partner? A review of the literature. *Globalization and Health, 9*(1), 38. doi: 10.1186/1744-8603-9-38.

Kiernan, P., O'Dempsey, T., Kwalombota, K., Elliott, L., & Cowan, L. (2011). Evaluation of effect on skills of GP trainees taking time out of programme (OOP) in developing countries. *Education for Primary Care: An Official Publication of the Association of Course Organisers, National Association of GP Tutors, World Organisation of Family Doctors, 25*(2), 78–83.

King, R., & Ruiz-Gelices, E. (2003). International student migration and the European 'year abroad'; effects on European identity and subsequent migration behaviour. *International Journal of Population Geography, 9,* 229–252.

Kolb, D. (1983). *David A. Kolb on Experiential Learning.* www.infed.org/biblio/b-explrn.htm, (pp. 1–11). Retrieved from www.infed.org/biblio/b-explrn.htm.

Leather, A. J. M., Butterfield, C., Peachey, K., Silverman, M., & Sheriff, R. S. (2010). International health links movement expands in the United Kingdom. *International Health, 2*(3), 165–171. doi: 10.1016/j.inhe.2010.04.004.

Lee, A. C. K., Hall, J. A., & Mandeville, K. L. (2011). Global public health training in the UK: Preparing for the future. *Journal of Public Health*, *33*(2), 310–316. doi: 10.1093/pubmed/fdr018.

Lewis, D. (2006). Globalization and international service: A development perspective. *Voluntary Action*. Institute for Volunteering Research. Retrieved from http://eprints.lse.ac.uk/14999/.

Lintern, S. (2013). NHS to face chronic nurse shortage by 2016. *Nursing Times* 18.

Longstaff, B. (2012). How international health links can help the NHs workforce. *International Health Links Centre*. http://www.hsj.co.uk/how-international-health-links-can-help-the-nhs-workforce-develop/5044915.fullarticle. Accessed 09 March 2016.

Lovett, W., & Gidman, J. (2011). Reflecting on the learning experiences of student nurses in rural Uganda. *British Journal of Community Nursing*, *16*(4), 191–195. doi: 10.12968/bjcn.2011.16.4.191.

Lumb, A., & Murdoch-Eaton, D. (2014). Electives in undergraduate medical education: AMEE guide no. 88. *Medical Teacher*, *36*, 557–572. doi: 10.3109/0142159X.2014.907887.

Lumley, L. (2011). *Doctors leaving New Zealand: Analysis of online survey results*. Medical Council of New Zealand.

Mahroum. (2000). Highly skilled globetrotters: The international migration of human capital. *R & D Management*, *30*(1), 23–32.

Malich, G., Coupland, R., Donnelly, S., & Baker, D. (2012). A proposal for field-level medical assistance in an international humanitarian response to chemical, biological, radiological or nuclear events. *Emergency Medicine Journal*, *30*, 10.

Marçal-Grilo, J. (2014). Sharing skills in dementia care with staff overseas. *Nursing Older People*, *26*(4), 35–39. doi: 10.7748/nop2014.04.26.4.35.e569.

Marsick, V. J., & Volpe, M. (1999). The nature and need for informal learning. *Advances in Developing Human Resources*, *1*(3), 1–9. doi: 10.1177/152342239900100302.

McCulloch, P., & Mishra, A. (2009). The effects of aviation-style non-technical skills training on technical performance and outcome in the operating theatre. *Health Care*, *18*(2), 109–115.

Medical Research Council. (2008). *Developing and evaluating complex interventions: New guidance*. London: Medical Research Council.

Meusberger, P. (2009). Spatial mobility of knowledge: A proposal for a more realistic communication model. *The Planning Review*, *177*(2), 29–39.

Mezirow, J. (1997). Transformative learning: Theory to practice. *New Directions for Adult and Continuing Education*, *74*, 5–12.

Moore, P., Surgenor, M., Ackers-Johnson, J., & Kakulgulu, P. (2015). SVP risk assessment report. https://www.uhsm.nhs.uk/about/education/programmes/global-health-learning-programme/.

Moyo, D. (2009). *Dead aid. Why aid is not working and how there is another way for Africa.* London: Penguin.

National Health Service. (2016). *NHS Workforce Statistics, September 2015, England, Experimental.* http://content.digital.nhs.uk/catalogue/PUB20335. Accessed 12 October 2016.

National Health Service and Department of Health. (2010) *The framework for NHS involvement in international development.* London: International Division.

National Health Service Digital. (2016). *Healthcare workforce statistics.* England: NHS Digital. http://content.digital.nhs.uk/catalogue/PUB21783/nhs-staf-sep-2015-mar-2016-rep.pdf. Accessed 5 October 2016.

National Health Service Electronic Staff Record (ESR) Data warehouse. Staff in post. Accessed 02 February 2013.

National Health Service Employers. (2016). *International recruitment.* http://www.nhsemployers.org/your-workforce/recruit/employer-led-recruitment/international-recruitment. Accessed 11 October 2016).

National Health Service England. (2014). https://www.england.nhs.uk/wp-content/uploads/2014/10/5yfv-web.pdf. Accessed 1 November 2016.

National Health Service Improvement. (2016). Agency rules, NHS. www.improvement.nhs.uk.

Ng, K., Van, D. L., & Ang, S. (2009). From experience to experiential learning: Cultural intelligence as a learning capability for global leader development. *Academy of Management Learning & Education, 8*(4), 511–526.

Nonaka, I., & Takeuchi, H. (1995). *The knowledge-creating company: How Japanese companies create the dynamics of innovation.* Oxford: Oxford University Press.

Norton, D., & Marks-Maran, D. (2014). Developing cultural sensitivity and awareness in nursing overseas. *Nursing Standard, 28*(44), 39–43. doi: 10.7748/ns.28.44.39.e8417.

Nursing and Midwifery Council (2012). *Guidance on professional conduct for nursing and midwifery students.* Nursing and Midwifery Council https://www.city.ac.uk/__data/assets/pdf_file/0007/65536/Guidance-on-Professional-Conduct-for-Nursing-and-Midwifery-Students.pdf. Accessed 11 October 2016.

Nursing and Midwifery Council. (2015). The code: Professional standards of practice and behaviour for nurses and midwives. *Nursing and Midwifery Council,* 1–19. doi: 10.1016/B978-0-7506-8644-0.00003-4.

Opengart, R. (2002). Free agent learners: The new career model and its impact on human resource development. *International Journal of Lifelong Learning, 21*(3), 220–233.

Park, C., Lee, J., & Wilding, M. (2016). Distorted policy transfer? South Korea's adaptation of UK social enterprise policy. *Policy Studies, (Ahead-Of-Print),* 1–20.

Park, C., Wilding, M., & Chung, C. (2014). The importance of feedback: Policy transfer, translation and the role of communication. *Policy Studies, 35*(4), 397–412.

Patrick, F. (2011). *Handbook of research on improving learning and motivation through educational games: Multidisciplinary approaches.* London: IGI Global.

Peate, I. (2008). Nursing electives: An innovative and creative learning opportunity. *British Journal of Nursing, 17*(1), 40–43.

Petrick, I. J., & Juntiwasarakij, S. (2011). The rise of the rest: Hotbeds of innovation in emerging markets. *Research-Technology Management, 54*(4), 24–29.

Public Health England. (2016). *Health fit for the future – public health people: A review of the public health workforce.* London: Public Health England.

Richards, D. A. (2015). The complex interventions framework. In D A Richards & I R Hallberg (2015). (Eds.), *Complex Interventions in Health* (pp. 1–15). London: Routledge.

Rodger, S., Webb, G., Devitt, L., Gilbert, J., Wrightson, P., & McMeeken, J. (2008). Clinical education and practice placements in the allied health professions: An international perspective. *Journal of Allied Health, 37*(1), 53–62.

Rohs, F. R., & Langone, C. A. (1997). Increased accuracy in measuring leadership impacts. *Journal of Leadership & Organizational Studies, 4*(1), 150–158.

Royal College of Nursing. (2015). *Working with humanitarian organisations: A guide for nurses, midwives and health care professionals.* London: RCN.

Royal College of Nursing. (2015). *Frontline first runaway agency spending.* London: Royal College of Nursing.

Sadler-Smith, E., Allinson, C. W., & Hayes, J. (2000). Learning preferences and cognitive style: Some implications for continuing professional development. *Manage Learn, 31*, 239–256.

Sales, S. M. (1966). Supervisory style and productivity: Review and theory. *Personnel Psychology, 19*(3), 275–286. doi: 10.1111/j.1744-6570.1966.tb00303.x.

Schneeberger, C., & Mathai, M. (2015). Emergency obstetric care: Making the impossible possible through task shifting. *International Journal of Gynecology & Obstetrics, 131*, S6–S9.

Sherraden, M. S., Lough, B. J. & Mc Bride, A. M. (2008). Effects of international volunteering and service: Individual and institutional predictors. *Voluntas: International Journal of Voluntary and Nonprofit Organisations, 19*(4), 395–421.

Shrum, W. M., Duque, R. B., & Ynalvez, M. A. (2010). Outer space of science: A video ethnography of reagency in Ghana. In P. Meusburger, D. N. Livingstone, & H. Jöns (2010). (Eds.), *Geographies of science.* Heidelberg: Springer.

Sidduique, H. (2014, 26th January). Figures show extent of NHS reliance on foreign nationals. *The Guardian.*

Smetherham, C., Fenton, S., & Modood, T. (2010). How global is the UK academic labour market?. Globalisation. *Societies and Education, 8*(3), 411–428.

Smith, C., Pettigrew, L. M., Seo, H., & Dorward, J. (2012). Combining general practice with international work: Online survey of experiences of UK GPs. *JRSM Short Reports, 3*(7), 46. doi: 10.1258/shorts.2012.012054.

Standage, R., & Randall, D. (2014). The benefits for children's nurses of overseas placements: Where is the evidence?. *Issues in Comprehensive Pediatric Nursing, 37*(2), 87–102. doi: 10.3109/01460862.2014.880531.

Stephens, M. 2015. Changing student nurses values, attitudes and behaviours: A Meta ethnography of enrichement activities. *Nursing and Care, 5*(1), 320.

Strachan, P. (2009). Guidelines for sending volunteers on overseas placements. *The Humanitarian Resource Centre.* http://www.humanitariancentre.org/hub/public/HC%20library%20catalogue.htm. Accessed 14 March 2015.

Tooke, J. (2009). *Aspiring to excellence. Findings and final recommendations of the independent inquiry into modernising medical careers.* London: Aldridge Press.

Tourangeau, A.E, & McGilton, K. (2004). Measuring leadership practices of nurses using the leadership practices inventory. *Nursing Research, 53*(3), 182–189.

UK Aid. (2015). tackling global challenges in the national interest. *UK Aid.* https://www.gov.uk/government/uploads/.../ODA_strategy_final_web_0905.pdf. Accessed 1 November 2016.

UKFPO. (2013). United Kingdom foundation programme. http://www.foundationprogramme.nhs.uk/pages/home. Accessed 3 November 2016.

Vygotsky, L. S., & Rieber, R. W. (1988). *The collected works of LS Vygotsky: Volume 1: Problems of general psychology, including the volume thinking and speech (vol. 1).* Berlin: Springer Science & Business Media.

Waugh, A., Smith, D., Horsburgh, D., & Gray, M. (2014). Towards a values-based person specification for recruitment of compassionate nursing and midwifery candidates: A study of registered and student nurses' and midwives' perceptions of prerequisite attributes and key skills. *Nurse Education Today, 34*(9), 1190–1195. doi: 10.1016/j.nedt.2013.12.009.

Williams, A., & Baláž, V. (2008). *International migration and knowledge.* London: Routledge.

Wright, J., Silverman, M., & Sloan, J. (2005). NHS links: A new approach to international health links. *Careerfocus, 330*(7488), 78–79.

Yule, S., Flin, R., Paterson-Brown, S., & Maran, N. (2006). Non-technical skills for surgeons in the operating room: A review of the literature. *Surgery, 139*(40), 140–149.

Zedtwitz, M. et al. (2015). A typology of reverse innovation. *Journal of Product Innovation Management, 32*(1), 12–28.

# INDEX

**L**

Leadership, 8, 34, 35, 44–53, 56, 58, 88
Legitimisation, 110
Length of stay, 16, 26–29, 74,
  95–98, 113
Levels, 6, 17, 23, 30, 33–34, 39, 44,
  58, 67, 79, 81, 86
Life-changing, 31
Lifelong learning, 2, 4, 32, 33, 93–95
Line manager, 8, 50, 69, 75, 76, 83, 95
Liverpool-Mulago Partnership
  (LMP), 115–119
Lobbying, 106
Location, 1, 11n4, 19–20, 22, 23, 33,
  54, 60, 61, 86, 92, 100, 104,
  117, 119
Loss, 74, 85
Low and middle income countries
  (LMICs), 2
Low-income countries, 86

**M**

Macklow-Smith, A., 5, 45, 58, 62
Maintenance role, 33
Management skills, 45, 48, 92
Manager, 6–8, 42, 46, 48, 50, 53, 54,
  67, 69, 75, 76, 83, 86, 95, 106, 119
Marks-Maran, D., 35, 57, 60
Marsick, V.J., 65
Measurement, 92
Measuring the Outcomes of
  Volunteering for Education
  (MOVE) study, 9
Medical Defence Union (MDU), 107
Medical leadership competency
  framework (MLCF), 45
Medical Protection Society (MPS), 106
Medical School, 9, 110
Medical students, 63, 81, 83
Medical training, 18, 29
Mental health, 42

Mentoring, 43, 63, 70, 105, 116
Meusberger, P., 92, 96
Mezirow, J., 31
Midwives, 18, 21, 22, 26, 63, 73,
  84, 87–88, 95, 107, 109, 112,
  115, 116
Migration, 2, 3, 7, 70, 80, 95
Mobilisation, professional
  voluntarism, 34–35
Mobility, international, 1–11, 14
Mobility metrics, 94–95
Mobility role, 33
Motivation, 2–4, 20, 35, 70, 92,
  93, 102
MOVE project, 17, 50, 56, 65n1, 68,
  88, 91, 93, 107n1, 111
MOVE survey, 123–124
Multiple placement experiences, 29
Multi Professional Education and
  Training (MPET), 33
mzungu (language), 61, 85, 89n8

**N**

Narrative, 63, 82, 85, 112
National Health Service (NHS), 1–11,
  13–30, 33–34, 49, 60, 76, 94
age group and length of stay, 27–29
cadre, 4, 15, 16, 22, 29
career mobility, 6–9
career stage, 44
costs and risks, 67–68
eight standard employment
  cadres, 15
gender, 20–22
international mobility and
  learning, 1–11
international placements, 1–11
length of stay, 26–27
MOVE study, 10
multiple placement experiences, 29
nationality, 23–24

Printed by Printforce, the Netherlands